D1100694

Marriage

With Marriage in Mind

With Marriage in Mind

A Discussion Program

Urban G. Steinmetz

FIDES PUBLISHERS INC.
NOTRE DAME, INDIANA

© Copyright: 1968, Fides Publishers Inc.

Notre Dame, Indiana

Library of Congress Catalog Card Number: 68-31774

Cover photo by Ed Lettau

Contents

A# 208

Chapter I

Using the Program Effectively

THIS IS A DIFFERENT KIND OF MARRIAGE TEXTBOOK. IT talks about marriage as it really is. As far as we know, nothing is concealed or glossed over.

It is not a "study" of marriage. You will find few statistics in this book because we do not feel that statistics are completely honest. They are often used to "prove" a point, when really there is not very much that anyone can prove about marriage. We know too little about it. For example, you have all heard that "Fifty percent of teenage marriages end in divorce." Most textbooks use this statistic in some form to show that teenage marriages are not workable. But what about the other fifty percent? We personally know a lot of people who were married and stayed married in their teens, and a few of them have built a beautiful life together.

Some statistics tend to compare everything to a norm; to give the impression that a certain kind of activity is "normal." This creates two problems. One is that the people who don't fit into their nice, neat categories feel that they are "abnormal," and they worry about it. The second is that married people tend to use statistics to get rid of their responsibilities. When things go wrong, they tend to say, "Oh, well, we are just like everybody else."

Finally, we do not really believe that people pay much attention to statistics. These are about "other" people who live in other parts of the country. The only kind of statistics that mean very much to us are the ones that we compile ourselves. You can do this easily by taking a careful and honest look at the people around you.

We will not be quoting the "experts" in this program, simply because we do not believe that there are any experts. Like the rest of us, psychiatrists, psychologists, sociologists, and family life specialists also have many problems in coping with the sometimes strange, always complicated human being they are married to.

There are no pat formulas or easy answers to marriage. Living with a person of the opposite sex is a tough, confusing, very real task that can be beautiful—but only if you make it beautiful. We cannot accept the fact that some people are doomed to failure because of their background. We believe that everyone can have a good marriage if he is willing to prepare for it and work at it.

There are only two ways to learn about marriage. One is the route that most of your parents took. We fall in love, get married, and then make the same mistakes that everyone else made before we fall in love again. You can judge this method for yourself simply by looking around you at the number of divorces.

Perhaps even more important are the number of couples that you know who live in a sort of armed truce "for the sake of the kids."

This is why we call this book a "program" rather than a "course" or a "text." There is a better way of preparing for marriage, but it is going to require a lot more of you than just reading. The method is simple: to listen to and to learn from the people who are living it.

The trick is to look deeply. We think that when you do you will decide that marriage is not just a honeymoon. It is loving sex when you love, and hating sex when you hate. It is dirty diapers and vomiting children and weeks of tension and jealousy over the guys and girls you used to go with. It is a real lover who belches at the table or snores in bed or complains about his hemorrhoids. It is looking at the person you want to change and realizing that she is not going to change, and it is facing this person for forty years across a breakfast table. With all of this, it is also comfort and love and the excitement of creating people who know how to love. It is the way that most of us freely choose to live.

Because marriage is forever and is the most intense and prolonged emotional contact that you will ever experience, the three decisions that will be facing you are probably going to be the most important ones you will ever make in your life.

The first one is *if* you should marry. We hope that you will give this one a lot of thought. It is just as illogical to marry because all of your friends are marrying as it is to join a convent because Sister Jane is so sweet. Some people need to be married; some people need to be single. Both are normal people.

The second decision is *who* you should marry. One of the worst experiences of a marriage counselor is to face people, across the desk, who married because they were "in love," and then wake up a few weeks later to discover that they didn't even know each other. Their decision to marry was based upon the fact that "we felt so good when we were with each other." They were perfectly compatible when they were together; they both liked to neck. We hope that your observations will help you to understand that boys always "feel good" to girls, and that girls always "feel good" to boys.

Finally, you will have to decide *when* you are ready for marriage. We hope you will decide to base this decision on a real knowledge of what marriage is all about, and on an honest analysis of your own maturity. You are no longer children. When you will be emotionally ready is a decision only you can make.

Marriage is for grown-ups; it's never for children. The reason so many couples fail, and so many more live in a sort of armed truce, is that they haven't grown up at all. They are 30-, 40-, or 50-year-old children. They haven't bothered to study marriage, and in some cases haven't discovered the simple facts of their own sexuality. They do not really communicate because they have never learned how to talk with each other. They live in a miserable dream world of personal hurt, constantly hoping that somehow love will come to them.

These people are not to be blamed. Most of them learned about marriage from parents who had never figured it out themselves. Blessed into marriage with a five-minute talk on prayer, their "knowledge" came from soap operas, movies, and dirty little books on sex. This was all of the preparation that was available to most of the people of your parents' generation, the one that Jeanette and I also belong to.

Many of us muddled through, and some of us managed to build a relationship that is beautiful. But even for those of us who did, ten, fifteen, or even twenty years were often wasted in useless struggle and bitterness. We had no idea of who we were, or how to go about being married. The constant cry that we hear in our *Marriage Enrichment Program* which points out this dilemma, is, "I wish we could have had this program ten years ago."

This is the opportunity that this program offers you. We will share with you everything that we have learned about marriage from over 1,000 counseling cases and from countless thousands of couples who have experienced the *Marriage Enrichment Program*. The rest will be up to you. You can casually read this book, get a good grade, and forget about it. If you do, you will just have to muddle through marriage like the rest of us did. There is no magic in the book.

Your second alternative is to use this program to really take stock of yourselves and learn everything you can about marriage. At times, this will be painful. You will discover that marriage is a very real experi-

ence, and that you are very human. You will want to
ask yourselves some honest questions about yourself
and give yourself some honest answers.

It also means work. The *Observe* portion of each
chapter suggests that you select five couples whom you
know personally and study them carefully all through
the program. These couples should be as different as
they can be; people who are married twenty or more
years as well as people who are married only one; families with a lot of children and families that are very
small. It will not be necessary to ask these couples questions; as a matter of fact, it will be better if they do not
know they are being observed. Just get the feel of them
when you are around them; how they operate, how they
treat each other; whether there is tension between them
or whether there is peace and love.

You will want to compare what you observe with the
experiences of the thousands of couples who are responsible for the material in this book. You will want to
weigh what you read here against what you see and
feel. From all of these things, you will want to start
to look over your own feelings about the people around
you; about love, sex, and marriage.

The *Observe* portion also suggests that you take a
hard look at the young people you come in contact
with. A very important part of the maturing process is
to accept yourself. We all feel very much alone at times,
and think that our worries and concerns are unique.
It helps a great deal to know that the boys and girls
you know best are fighting many of the same personal
battles. Observing them and getting the "feel" of them

is the best way of developing the understanding and the tolerance of people that any successful marriage requires.

Finally, you are going to have to make a decision on discussion. If you have done your reading and observing, good discussion will come naturally. To a large extent, marriage *is* communication. If you can talk to each other openly, honestly, and about everything, your marriage will be a success. The discussion section should be a real communications laboratory—but only if you decide to do your homework. There is no real point in sharing ignorance.

Those of you who want to shift the responsibility of discussion to the teacher are likely to be badly disappointed. Do not expect your teacher to be an expert on marriage, even though he may have had a course or two —or even a degree—in family relations. No matter what his training, he is not a person who can give you nice pat answers that will work for you. At best, he will be a person who has some ideas to share that are well worth listening to. He will learn as much from you and your observations as you will learn from him.

This is probably the first program that attempts to involve all of the people who are concerned about you and your marriage. Your parents and teachers are going to be asked to join you in a total approach. If it works the way we would like to see it work, your parents will be reading and talking at home at the same time that you are reading and talking at school.

All of our work at the Family Life Bureau is with teachers, parents, and young adults. All of it is in some way related to marriage. The first question that we always receive from your parents is "How do we communicate with our teens?" The first question that we receive from young people, on the other hand, is "How do we communicate with our parents?" We hope that this program will be a partial answer for both of you. Some of you may have very good communications at home. Some of you may not be able to communicate at all. Everyone's communications can stand some improvement. I hope that you will start out with the idea that your parents do want to talk with you, even if it doesn't seem that way at times.

Some of your parents are going to be something less than wildly enthusiastic about this new program. It's not that they don't care or that they don't want to become involved with you; it's simply that we're all afraid to really examine ourselves. Parents are people, and they're no different than young people. Many times we like to pretend that things are going along just fine and we're afraid of what will happen if we try to change them.

Parents, too, are afraid of honesty, particularly in the sexual area. They're going to need a great deal of help and encouragement from you if this program is going to succeed.

If you have had some problems in openly talking with your parents or teachers, this is a good time to tell them about it. It does little good for parents to say, "Why can't I talk to my teenager?" and for teenagers to say, "Why can't I talk to my parents?" if no one does much to change things. This program is a real opportunity for all of you to get everything out on the table where you can look at it and discuss it fully.

We are going to talk a great deal about responsibility. You are young adults. This is your life; you are responsible for what happens to it. No one can tell you what to do with your life or with your marriage. If you want to change the things that are wrong with your life now and if you want to prepare for a solid and happy marriage in the future, we have given you the tools to work with.

OBSERVE

This is the only *Observe* that will be at the end of a chapter. From now on, the *Observe* portion will have to be your homework.

Your first task is to get the "feel" of all the people who are involved with you in the program. A good place to start is with yourself. Probably you're a little afraid of this whole thing. Most of us are afraid of any new experience, especially when it involves taking a hard look at ourselves. Some of you may doubt whether it will ever be possible for you to talk to people that you hardly know about your real feelings on sex, love, and marriage.

It will probably help you to look around and notice that just about everyone else in the room is uncomfortable, too. Even your teacher is probably a little nervous. He or she is probably used to giving a lecture,

and that's much easier. In the handbook we've asked
your teacher to really be honest with you; and that's
not easy.

The other students will be easier to read because most
of them will feel a lot like you do. Probably most of the
girls are quite excited about starting a program of this
kind, but are a little bit afraid, too. Probably some of
the boys are acting indifferent or nonchalant. Why do
you think that boys feel that they have to act this way
when other boys and girls are around?

As you try to get the feel of the people around you
who are going to be involved with you in this program,
your parents may be the hardest of all. Sometimes you
may think it's impossible to talk to them about anything important. Try to understand your real feelings
about them. It helps a great deal if you admit to yourself and to them that you care about them and about
how they feel.

DISCUSS

It will help you get started in your discussion if you
simply talk about your feelings for a little while. If
you're a little uncomfortable about the whole thing,
say that you are. If you don't like it, say that, too.
Discussions always start better if everyone knows where
everyone else stands.

Classroom Discussion. The suggestions below are
there for you to use if you want to use them. Don't feel
that you have to talk about all of them, or even about

any of them, if there's something that seems to be more important to the members of the class. However, you're going to want to be careful with this. Things get tough when we start to talk about ourselves, so we naturally try to avoid it. If this program is going to work, all of you are going to have to watch out for getting side-tracked on some long discussion that doesn't have anything to do with what you should be talking about. A little humor can be a big help here; somebody saying something like, "Boy, we sure avoided that one, didn't we?"

The following suggestions should help to keep you on the track:

1. Will it be hard to talk about sex and marriage in a mixed group? Why?

2. Have you had much of an opportunity for serious discussion in the school? Why do you think this is?

3. What do you think of the *Observe* idea? Do you think most people really observe? Or, do most of us look at things and then tend to see what we want to see?

4. How do you think your parents are going to feel when you start observing them?

5. I hope that you will decide to talk about honesty. Do you think that your parents have been honest with you? Do you think your teachers have been honest with you? Are boys generally honest with girls? Are girls generally honest with boys? Are you honest with your friends, or do you often pretend so that they will like you?

Discussion at Home. The best way to begin discussion at home is to simply tell your parents about the new program and how you feel about it. Normally, young people don't tell their parents much about what goes on at school. This is a good time to start. Tell them about what happened in the discussion and about some of the things that were said. Keep in mind that it may be just as hard for them to start talking about this as it is for you. If it starts a little hard, don't get angry this time. Be patient, and let them know how important it is for you to talk to them.

I hope that you will nag them a little bit, too, about doing their homework and keeping up with you in the class. This program is going to work best if everybody gets completely involved and stays completely involved. We're all a little human and we're all a little lazy and we're all a little afraid. Older adults are no different from young adults. When we've got things that are hard to do, we all put them off if we can.

Chapter II

The Simple Act
of Sexual Intercourse

OBSERVE

SELECT FIVE COUPLES OF DIFFERENT AGES THAT YOU KNOW
quite well. These may be parents of friends, relatives,
or an older brother and sister. Start now to get the feel
of these couples and their relationship to each other.
Here are some things you may want to look for:

1. Is there generally a relaxed and comfortable feeling when the two of them are together? Is there tension?
Do they seem proud of each other?

2. Do they discuss sex in the same way that they
would discuss anything else? Do they tell jokes about
it or are they embarrassed about it?

OBSERVE II

Select three friends who are not in this classroom.
Mention casually that you are discussing sexual intercourse. You can learn a great deal about their feelings
by how they respond—

1. Do they ask you many questions? If they do, they probably feel they need the knowledge.

2. Are they very casual about the whole thing? Sometimes this can mean that they are quite well informed, but more often it means that they like to pretend that they're informed.

3. Do they quickly change the subject? They may be afraid to discuss it.

4. Do they tell crude jokes about sex? What do you think that this means?

5. Do your friends tend to laugh very easily at any sexual remark, even if it isn't funny?

Putting sex
in perspective

It may seem odd to many of you to talk about sexual intercourse so close to the beginning of a book on marriage. Many people have probably told you to forget about sex; that it is not important and that certainly you shouldn't be thinking about it at your age. They may have even urged you to get rid of your "impure thoughts" and to pray when such thoughts strike you.

As a matter of fact, it is almost impossible for anyone living today to completely forget about sex for very long. Some of the younger college people have said that our generation is "all hung up on sex," and they are certainly right. We would like to think that the young adults of today are putting sex in its proper perspective, but apparently they are just as "hung up" as we representatives of your parents' generation. Just a few weeks ago our staff conducted a complete marriage program in a CCD course at a local Catholic high school. Although only about fifteen percent of the material we presented was on sex, all of the questions that we received from the students were in some way related to this subject.

If any of us did really succeed in entirely forgetting about sex, we would be lost as soon as we turned on the T.V., walked into a local news depot or bookstore, or went to a movie. Sex is before us constantly. It is used to sell automobiles, makeup and hair dressing, and almost every other piece of merchandise that we buy. It is woven all through our current literature and is instantly available in even such conservative strongholds as our local libraries.

We are not going to escape from sex, and are certainly not going to be able to avoid thinking about it. Thoughts about sex are a natural, normal part of everyone's existence. They are put there by God for what to me is a very beautiful purpose: to attract men and women to each other so that eventually we may hope to build strong, loving marriages.

Since we cannot either bury sex or put it away from us, the best thing that all of us can do is to face our feelings honestly and know how to handle them and what to do with them. This is not easy in a generation that is so obsessed with sex and at the same time so afraid of it that we do not even know how to talk about it to our young people. After all, it is not the youth of today who are writing the movies, the pornographic literature, and the Mustang ads; it is the people of my age—the stone-age generation—the people who have suffered with Puritanical ideas about sex most of their lives.

Most so-called adults are sure of only one thing regarding sex. We would like our young adults to have fewer problems with it than we did. We want you to have information, but in many cases we don't know quite what we want you to have. Probably you have already been exposed at home and in the classroom to the confusion of adults who honestly tried to tell you something about it, but who actually spent nearly all of their time beating around the bush and only succeeded in boring you and further arousing your curiosity. This is why sex sometimes becomes an obsession with young people. We have told you half-truths and talked all around the area without really telling you anything. In doing so, we have made it so big and so out of proportion that we probably have taught you to fear your own sexuality as we were afraid of ours; and, consequently, to think about it a great deal more than a healthy young adult normally would. We have told you that sex is sacred and that sex is beautiful and then we have added all kinds of "but's."

I am not apologizing for our generation, because in spite of the fact that we have probably left you thoroughly confused, we have done a far better job than the generation before us or the generation before that. At least today our feelings and confusions are coming out in the open, and young people of today are approaching it much more honestly. Sexually, we are beginning to mature.

For all of the reasons listed above, it is necessary when talking about marriage to get into the sexual area immediately, answer your questions as best we can, and get the facts of sexual intercourse behind us. I have kept insisting that you are young adults, and I thoroughly believe this. If we are to ask you to make responsible sexual decisions, these decisions must be based on a complete understanding of yourselves as sexual people. We believe that it will be a relief to you to discover that sex is not such a big thing after all, and that once you discover why you feel as you do and why you have so many doubts and confusions, we can move on to talk intelligently about love and marriage.

God intended the act of sexual intercourse to be a simple thing. As He designed it, it is almost a foolproof method of totally loving and possessing each other. Given enough love, the process of sexual intercourse in marriage should be an automatic one.

But human beings have always had a real ability to alter the simplicity and beauty of creation. In order to get the sexual act back into perspective, we have to look at it as it is and as it is meant to be: a natural, normal, instinctive act of loving each other completely. Because you have already been exposed to many half-truths and to a great deal of misinformation, we may have to bore some of you by talking about the whole process as if you knew nothing about it.

The part of the male that is most important in sexual intercourse is the penis. This is a finger-like part of the body that hangs between the legs and is normally soft and pliable. Immediately below the penis is a sac of skin containing two testicles which are football-shaped and about the size of a large marble.

During the process of loving and holding each other in marriage, the penis becomes hard and firm and stretches somewhat. When this happens, the mind of the man focuses almost automatically on sexual intercourse, and his desire to possess his wife becomes very strong.

In a similar position between the legs of the woman lies the vagina. This is a small opening designed to receive and hold the man's penis. When the woman is held and caressed, this vagina should become lubricated so that the penis of the man can be inserted quite easily.

In the normal process of sexual intercourse, the married man and woman begin by just simply treating each other decently all through their married lives. This leads to a feeling of closeness and love, which again leads to lovemaking, holding, kissing, and caressing. The emotions of the couple rise to the point at which they want to totally possess each other, and finally the hard, firm penis of the male is inserted into the vagina of the female, which has been lubricated through love to receive it.

If the couple are grown up and mature, the strong feelings that occur during the act of sexual intercourse are very difficult to describe. There is a sense of almost total love and total beauty that perhaps cannot be achieved any place else in life. The expression that we hear very often is that they want to "eat each other up," but this doesn't describe it very well. The body temperature of both male and female rises; the excitement of the two people greatly increases; heartbeat and pulse quicken. As the penis moves within the vagina, all of these feelings intensify. In nearly every case, the male climaxes. (What this means is that the penis gives off a white milky fluid containing sperm in quick little bursts and then fully relaxes.) At the same time his excitement disappears rather quickly, and if it has been an act of love, there is a feeling of almost complete contentment.

Sometimes a woman also climaxes. If she has been loved enough, this climax may be even more intense than it is in the man. With the woman, however, the climax is essentially a relaxing thing that gives her very strong feelings of contentment and love. The pitch of excitement drops rather suddenly and then more slowly subsides until she arrives at a feeling of almost total relaxation and well-being.

The process of reaching this climax in both the male and female is again a very simple and uncomplicated thing. Because they love each other, the couple simply does what they instinctively want to do: They hold and caress each other.

Every female is equipped with a set of sexual triggers which the man very naturally wants to hold and caress during the process of lovemaking. Physically, these triggers are the breasts, which the man may caress or kiss; the lips, and here quite often the couple engages in French kissing; the clitoris, which is a very sensitive area which lies at the top of the vagina and generally moves against the penis in sexual intercourse; and the vagina, which the man normally plays with prior to sexual intercourse.

The woman, too, generally wants to totally possess her man because she loves him. The process of preparing him for sexual intercourse is very simple and natural. While they are preparing each other for the act, she responds very strongly to his kissing and caressing, and she naturally and lovingly holds and caresses the penis and the testicles of the man.

Again, the position of sexual intercourse is natural, normal, and simple. Because we love each other very much, we hold each other. Because we want to increase our feelings of love, we press our bodies against each other with the sensitive areas of both man and woman in very close contact. The breasts of the woman rest against the chest of the man. The lips are in contact, and during the act the penis moves against the clitoris. The excitement that we create in each other does the rest.

These are the physical facts of sexual intercourse. There are no problems here. If two people who knew nothing at all about sex were placed on a desert island and came to love each other very deeply, they would discover the mechanics of sex in a matter of moments. They would never experience any problem with technique as long as they continued to love each other and talk to each other honestly.

Our problem with sex is our so-called "knowledge" of sex. We have been taught so many things that are phony and false about the techniques, positions, and mechanics that we have to "unlearn" most of them before we can begin to love each other.

When we see the number of books by learned doctors that describe in great detail the positions and techniques of sex, it is no wonder that adults of all ages are confused. To people who have achieved a mature appreciation of married sexuality, these books are almost amusing and a little pathetic. The unfortunate part of these so-called "marriage manuals" is that millions of unhappy people look to these "scientists" for guidance. This is why we hear a lot of nonsense about "sexual adjustment" and "sexual compatibility." It is why we hear some cynical young people say, "You don't buy a car without trying it out."

But sexual intercourse is not a matter of practice, experience, or technique. It is a matter of love and maturity. The problems are not physical problems. They are related to how we have been taught to feel about sex, how we feel about ourselves, and how we feel about each other. In other words, it is simple, decent, human treatment that makes sex in marriage a beautiful thing. Selfishness, immaturity, misunderstanding, and fear make it terrible. We are not machines that need to be adjusted; we are people who need to be loved.

DISCUSS

Classroom Discussion. This discussion is not going to be easy. It's very early in the course to talk about sex in a mixed group. Quite a few of you are going to be embarrassed. Some of you will not be ready to talk at all. None of this is bad; have patience with yourselves and with each other. Probably some of you are tempted to suggest that the boys go into one room and the girls go into another for your discussion. This isn't going to help much, although it would be easier to talk in an all-boy or an all-girl group. However, you're not going to find out how the other sex thinks and feels if you both get off in separate groups, are you?

Very few of you will want to discuss the physical facts of sexual intercourse. More important are your attitudes and feelings. Since it's always easier to talk about other people than it is to talk about ourselves, a good place to start is with the people that you have observed.

One word of caution. Please do not use any names or other kind of identification when you're talking about other people. This is just simple courtesy and respect for the individual.

Couples That You Have Observed

1. Did there seem to be a comfortable feeling between them? Or, did you notice a great deal of bitterness and sarcasm?

2. Were there little signals that passed between them? Private jokes that they thoroughly enjoyed? Or, was there tension? Were they short with each other? Did they tend to avoid each other and each go his own way?

Your Friends

1. What kind of knowledge do your friends seem to have? Where did they get this knowledge?

2. Are they able to talk freely about sex?

3. If your friends tell dirty jokes, why do you suppose they do this?

4. Why do you suppose that so many million American women are all absorbed in soap operas? Why do so many men and women read sexy magazines? Are they really interesting or is there some kind of a hang-up?

Yourself

1. What kind of sex education did you have?

2. How did you feel about receiving it in this way?

Discussion at Home

We don't like to offer explicit suggestions about how to talk with your parents. You know them better than we do. You know whether you can approach them directly, or whether an open discussion is something that you're going to have to build up to over a period of time. Again, we would strongly suggest that you are careful not to avoid discussion.

You can break the ice by simply telling them about the discussion that you had in school. It will be comforting to them to hear about your friends' reactions. Most parents feel a little bit guilty over the fact that they haven't discussed this matter as fully as they would have liked. It makes them feel good to know that they're not the only parents who have the same problem.

Finally, when talking with your parents, don't forget the most important part of any discussion: listening. Be patient; it may be hard for them to start.

Chapter III

The Boy Matures

OBSERVE

THE IMPORTANT PART OF THIS *Observe* IS TO ONCE AGAIN try to get the feel of the men that you know. First of all, look carefully at the husbands in the couples that you are observing. Here are some of the things that will be talked about in the chapter:

1. Confidence in self.
2. Responsibility. Does the man that you are observing try to shift responsibility for the things that he does onto his wife? Does he blame other people for things that are obviously his own fault? Or, does he assume responsibility himself for the things that he does?
3. How does the husband treat his wife and his daughters? Does he run them down and constantly criticize them? Does he build them up? Does he seem to have a real respect for women?
4. How does this man demonstrate his masculinity? If he is always boasting and bragging, it may mean that he really has very little self-respect and confidence in himself. Does he seem to have a healthy respect for

31

sex? Or, is he always talking about it with a dirty mouth or in a hurting kind of way?

OBSERVE II

The second place that you can explore what masculinity means to different people is to take a look at your male friends. Try to observe at least three of them:

1. Many young adults, as well as many old adults, try to prove themselves by showing off, bragging, reckless driving, rudeness to other people, and so on. Try to look a little deeper than what you see on the surface. If one of the people that you are observing does these things, does he really have confidence in himself?

2. Do you find that the young men you are observing act differently in different areas? That in some areas they have no confidence in themselves at all while in other areas they have a great deal of confidence? Why do you think this is?

3. What kind of conversations do they have about sex? Do they respect sex or downgrade it? How do they seem to regard themselves as sexual people?

4. Can you talk honestly about real feelings to these friends? Do they try to hide their feelings? Do they pretend that they have no problems?

Manliness means responsibility

As a forty-seven year old man who is still trying to discover what maturity means, I feel very strongly that this chapter has to be something more than simply recounting the facts and feelings that a young man has as he begins to mature. Becoming a man is a very rough job and one that doesn't end at any magical age such as twenty-one or even fifty-nine. When manhood starts to happen, a boy needs something to hold onto; some guidelines that will help him face not only the physical changes that are taking place in his body but also the more important things that are happening in his mind. This is why I would like to share with you some of the things that I have discovered in my own search for manhood.

I am afraid that I don't believe very much in "success," "life-adjustment," or even in "getting along with other people." More important to me is what the philosophers call "peace of soul." I would say it more simply than this. The thing that makes my life worth living is that most of the time I can look at myself and like what I see.

This is what manliness means to me. It's not an easy thing to achieve because it means that you will be working on it all of your lives. At times it seems that the whole world is working against you. It seems to want

to make you feel guilty and afraid. It encourages you
to find an easier path to happiness.

Every single person in this world is trying to find
contentment within himself, and the great bulk of us
clearly recognize the only way we can discover it is by
making a contribution to others. Yet we men are constantly searching for an easier path; trying to ignore
the fact that we largely create our own heavens and
hells. We always want to blame others for our own
failures.

Probably the first time that the young man starts to
recognize what manhood really means is in his early
teens. Up until this time he doesn't face very much of
anything. His parents are bad or good, and in either
case he loves them. He believes in them even when
they are not very believable people. Because he is a
child, he makes excuses for all of the people that he
loves. He pretends that they are what he wants them
to be, and confidently hopes that tomorrow they will
be different.

But in his teens the boy is slowly faced with the fact
of manhood. It starts very slowly with the growth of
whiskers on his chin, hair under his arms and around
the penis and testicles. Pimples appear on his face and
neck and his voice cracks and deepens. The genital
organs have been an unimportant part of his body until now, but slowly their message begins to be heard:
"You are not a boy anymore. You'd better start thinking about what it means to become a man because
physically you are becoming a man."

The physical process of changing from a boy to a man is called puberty. Because people are very different it happens to different boys at different ages. Some boys begin the process as early as ten or eleven; some as late as sixteen or seventeen. All of them are perfectly normal. Science has never fully determined why these differences exist but to me the answer is simple. People are different. Some have black hair; some have brown hair. All of these are normal, too.

The whole process of growing up can be a wonderful, challenging thing. All little boys want to be men and it should be a great thing to be able to say "finally we are arriving." Generally, however, it is not great because so many people have put doubts and fears into our minds about what is taking place.

During most of the years of his life, the penis of the boy hangs soft and unnoticed between his legs. When he is very small, it sometimes stands erect, but this is caused by pressure on the bladder. Now as he matures, the erection of the penis is associated with how he thinks and acts, and sometimes this bothers him.

The erection of the penis is common to all young men, and it will occur at times all during their lives. The biological process behind this erection is in itself a very interesting one, but one that doesn't concern us here. It is, however, an important part of the whole process of understanding why we act as we do, and we would certainly suggest that all of you will want to explore it. Any good biology text will show you the detailed functions of the various glands and organs

that are a part of the whole process of erection, ejacu-
lation, and sexual intercourse.

The part that we are concerned with here is that the
penis becomes hard and firm, and the thing that triggers this erection is the mind. This makes it a sexual
erection because it is now associated with thoughts and
feelings about sex. Nature is really trying to tell us
something with this first sexual erection: "You are becoming a man; you had better give some thought as to
what kind of a man you want to be."

With most of us, these first erections were very em-
barrassing. Somewhere along the line, almost everything sexual has been associated with sin, fear, or immoral excitement.

With some of us, these first few erections were a
terrifying thing, simply because we so-called "adults"
have made them so. In some homes, nothing sexual is
ever discussed. In some schools, the natural thoughts
of young men are called impure. Some women do not
understand the normal, natural functioning of the boy
and may have indicated to him in some way that the
appearance of an erection means that he is dirty-
minded. We see a lot of boys in counseling who have
developed some real problems centering around their
first erections.

Sexual feelings are very pleasant and exciting feelings in everyone. They should be; this is what attracts
us to each other and is one of the most important elements that contribute to the love of a man for a woman
and to the establishment of a loving home. But if we

have been taught that these feelings are bad, it causes us to feel guilty and can lead to problems. We certainly can't hide or discard our sexual thoughts and feelings; they are an important and natural part of every one of us. If we think to ourselves, "This is bad; I will not think about it anymore," we are simply kidding ourselves. The more that we try to suppress sexual feelings and pretend that they do not exist, the more the mind wants to focus on them, and the more erections are likely to occur.

The erection of the penis is simply an outward sign of other changes that are taking place within the body and the mind of the young adult. The testicles, football-shaped organs which hang in a sac called the scrotum and lie beneath the penis and between the legs of the male, now combine with other glands and organs to begin a manufacturing process which will last all through the man's life. The body manufactures semen, which is a white, sticky, milky fluid. It also manufactures sperm. Under a microscope, these sperm are extremely tiny fish-like organisms that will someday swim toward the ovum or egg of the female and join with it to become a new human being. Again, any good biology book will show you in detail how these processes work. Important to our understanding here is that semen serves as a carrier of the sperm and that both of these are constantly being supplied to the body.

Since semen and sperm are constantly being manufactured, there has to be a method of disposing of the surplus. One of these methods that we discussed in the last chapter is sexual intercourse, but even in marriage, this will not always take care of the available supply.

There are two other methods of disposing of the excess semen and sperm. The first of these is an automatic process which takes place when the boy is sleeping. The technical term used in describing this process is Nocturnal Emission, but the more common term and the one that we will use here is Wet Dream. The wet dream is very similar to any other dream of the human being. It is usually very confused and mixed up and generally has some sexual content. Just like any other dream, it is brought on because the person is sleeping restlessly or fitfully. In some young people, these wet dreams may happen once a night or even oftener. In others, they may occur as little as once a month or less. All of these variations are normal; they simply mean that some people dream a lot and some people don't. A few psychiatrists see great sexual significance in the frequency of wet dreams; most feel it is more closely related to the number of helpings of pizza that young men eat before bedtime. Quite often they occur in the morning when there is constant pressure on the bladder which focuses the mind on the penis.

The mechanics of the wet dream are simple. The sexual content of the dream causes the penis to stand erect. Quite often, but not always, there is some picture of intercourse in the mind. Any other stimulating experience can give the same kind of reaction. As the dream intensifies, so does the feeling of excitement in the penis. Finally orgasm occurs. This means that the erect penis gives off semen and sperm in short spurts and then relaxes.

Wet dreams happen to all males and everyone is aware of them. Because sexual feelings are a hidden thing in many homes, a great many teenage boys worry about their mothers finding a spot on their pajamas or bed. Their worry is unnecessary. Every mother, of course, is familiar with this process because her husband generally has this same experience all through his life. Sexual intercourse is not a substitute for wet dreams. If a man is tense and is not sleeping very well they can and do occur at any time.

The final method of disposing of semen and sperm is called masturbation. This means simply that the boy plays with the penis until it ejaculates or gives off semen and sperm. Like all sexual activity of any kind, this is an extremely exciting experience and one that every boy has some familiarity with.

Quite often the boy's first experience with masturbation begins with a wet dream. As the penis becomes erect and firm, he very naturally tends to place his hand on it. When he does, his excitement increases. In the twilight period between deep sleep and awakening, there is a kind of half-conscious time in which he may play with the penis and very thoroughly enjoy himself.

Some of you may have been taught that masturbation is a serious sin; that it tends to introvert the personality, or even that it can lead to sexual impotency.

All of these are symptoms of the fear with which the human race has surrounded all sexual activity in the past.

Masturbation is not that simple. Because every boy has an entirely different background and entirely different experiences, masturbation has a somewhat different meaning to every one of them.

Let's take a look at that boy who really has a masturbation problem. He's worried and upset about it and finds himself spending a great deal of time alone. He finds himself playing with his penis whenever he gets a chance. He feels very guilty, but the more he tries to put it out of his mind, the more masturbation becomes a problem for him.

This "bad" boy probably is not bad at all. If we look at the experiences that he has had with his own sexuality, we quickly come to understand that masturbation is a real hang-up or obsession with him. He has very little control over his behavior simply because he doesn't understand it. We have seen dozens of boys in counseling with this kind of a problem, and their past history almost always goes something like this: The boy starts into puberty with almost no sexual knowledge at all. He has no idea of what is going to happen to him, but has a vague idea that anything that is sexual is vaguely wrong and probably quite sinful. Sometimes he's criticized or teased by other students who don't understand what's happening to him either. At the same time, the erection of the penis gives him a feeling of pleasure.

Whenever we try to hide something from ourselves, or feel guilty about something, or don't fully understand something that we know is important to us, our minds immediately focus on it. The more guilty we feel and the less we know about it, the more we think about it. Since all of our sexuality is controlled by the brain, this naturally causes the boy to have more frequent erections than the normal boy would have. Erections, again, focus the boy's mind on sex, because with the erection of the penis comes pressure and thoughts relating to sex. The more we try to think of something else, the more, of course, our mind tends to focus on the penis.

Some boys start masturbating in a kind of desperation. They are simply so embarrassed that they feel they have to do something about the constant erections. They find that when they play with themselves until they finally ejaculate, the penis goes down and they have some relief. However, this relief is generally short. If the boy is guilty about his feelings to start with, the fact that he has completed masturbation again increases guilt, which again focuses the mind on the penis.

We might call this the masturbation trap. It can become dangerous and can cause a boy a lot of unnecessary worry. Like anything else that we feel guilty about, it may tend to disturb his whole life and focus his attention upon himself. It can lead to a boy's becoming introverted and completely avoiding other boys and girls.

It can also lead to homosexuality. Sometimes boys

who have this kind of problem and don't know what
to do about it tend to select friends with the same kind
of problem. It's very hard for anyone to keep on feeling
guilty about anything; especially if it's something that
he doesn't seem to be able to do anything about. As a
result, when the boys get together, they start talking
about their masturbation experiences in a bragging sort
of way. They compare themselves to each other. If they
are lonesome enough, it is not a very long step from this
point to the point at which they are playing with each
other's genital organs. This is the first step toward homosexuality. The guilty feelings that a boy has about this
kind of activity can cause him to completely avoid the
opposite sex and boys of his own sex who do not have
this problem. He finds himself more and more in the
company of boys that share his problem and very
shortly feels completely excluded by the other society.

Nearly all boys have some experience with masturbation. A great many have done some experimenting
with other boys. There are many reasons for this. One
is that all sexual feelings are powerful emotions, and
it's nearly impossible to always have them under control. But when it becomes a problem, it is almost always because someone has done a terrible job of teaching the boy about his sexuality. Since nearly every boy
has had some bad teaching, nearly every boy has some
problems.

Nearly every human problem can be solved if we
understand why it is a problem and do something constructive about it. The boy who occasionally mastur-
bates and feels guilty about it, can usually work out

the problems by himself, by simply reexamining everything that he knows about sex and where he got his knowledge. As he begins to understand his feelings and to realize that these feelings are a normal, healthy part of growing up, he becomes less concerned with them and the problem disappears.

For the boy with really serious problems that cause him a great deal of guilt and shame, more help may be needed. He is going to have to search out some adult that he can talk the whole thing through with. This is not always easy to do. There is a very good possibility that the first adult or two that he seeks out will be just as hung up on sex as he is. A lot of ridiculous advice is passed out to young people with masturbation problems. It ranges all the way from "take a cold shower" to "pray harder."

This is where the young man's responsibility for himself comes in. Every school and most homes will have some adult who is quite mature, has a wholesome attitude toward sex, and is a good listener. Every young man can locate this kind of person if he wants to.

Mature communications with God can be the best potential source of help with any sort of problem. The word mature is very important here. Immature people have an immature concept of God. They see Him as a mighty Being who is always ready to punish at the slightest sign of wrongdoing. They cannot recognize that this is the loving God who created them and who understands them thoroughly. It must be quite an insult to God to have people think of Him as one who is always ready to respond with swift and terrible pun-

ishment. Yet, this concept of a small god seems to go
hand in hand with a lot of severe problems in masturbation. Perhaps this is why so many people have such
terrible guilt.

It's far too simple to say that "masturbation is a sin"
or "masturbation is all right." The best word that I
can find to describe most masturbation problems is
unfortunate; perhaps *unnecessary* is even a better
word. Getting rid of the problem is simply a process
of straightening out our thinking on the whole area
of sexuality and reaching the point where we recognize our sexuality as good. An erection is a simple re-
minder to the boy that he is becoming a man; that he
has to start thinking about accepting the responsibilities of a man.

Yet the mixed-up picture of sexuality is only part
of the whole false picture of what masculinity means.
Our Hollywood image of a man is of a person who is
big, strong, and tough. He confides in no one. Even if
the image were true, it would be hard on the guy who
is little, physically weak, and emotionally tender. Yet,
he might be a lot more of a man than the tough guy
who gets all the credit for it.

The Hollywood concept of a man would be amusing
if it weren't so serious. The James Bond type is an example. Here is a person who is so unsure of his masculinity that he has to be proving it to himself twenty-
four hours a day by putting other people down. In his
frantic search for self identity, he shoots people, fights
everyone, seduces women, drives sexy cars (look at
me!). All of his relationships with people are hurting

relationships. He has to make other people little to make himself big.

This joke of a man is very serious indeed. It forces every boy to play "let's pretend" during most of his growing up life. The only way he can show his masculinity is by putting other people down. He has to drive faster than they do. He has to drink them under the table. He's got to squeal his tires louder on the corners; play chicken and make someone else give in. He's got to tell the other guys about how many girls he's made.

This image of a man is not only serious; it's deadly. There is nothing more unmasculine than putting another person down just to build yourself up. Yet a very large segment of our society has come to worship this kind of person. We see a man who is so unsure of himself that he has to climb the highest mountain, shoot the fastest rapids, and build a career out of walking over people. What happens? Obviously the man could use some help. Instead, we make him a national hero.

Largely because of this false picture of what masculinity means, many young men are forced to live in a brutal society. The hurting kind of sex that we see all around us grows and flourishes here. In order to be looked up to by the other boys, many young men have to prove to their friends that they are stronger than other people. They have to especially prove that they are stronger than women. Anything that helps the boy to prove his "strength" becomes "right." In this kind of jungle, the young man can use any kind of tactic in approaching a woman. The important thing is that he conquers her. A man can use the fact that a girl is a loving person. He can tell her of his great need for her, and even tell her how much he loves her and cares for her. Then, he can laugh at her because he has conquered her, and proven that she is the weaker sex.

It is little wonder that so many people rebel at this kind of phoniness. We know a great deal of what it really means to be a man, but we don't talk about it very much. It may help girls to understand boys a little better if they will recognize the terrible loneliness of the average young adult. In one way or another, he has been told so often that "you are a man; you have to stand on your own two feet" that he has a hard time confiding in anyone, even his close friends. In a very real sense, he doesn't dare confide. He may be laughed at if he does.

How does this concept of manliness measure up to the ideal of happiness that we're all looking for in our lives? I think you are all aware that when you push people, they push back. When you conquer people, they're resentful and hurt. Perhaps this false concept of masculinity helps to explain why the drunk tanks around the country are so loaded with football heroes, prize fighters, and warriors.

I would like to suggest a different concept of manliness. Think about it and talk it over in your class: A man is a person who knows what he is and likes what he is, because what he is is good. He accepts responsibility for the things that he does.

This man has a great deal of respect for all other people, even those who disagree with him. Our man has a particular respect for women. He recognizes that he is going to need one woman someday to complete him and that his happiness with her will depend upon plain, decent human treatment. He recognizes her capacity for love, and her dependence on him for love.

This man is honest. He doesn't pretend to be anybody. He is willing to hurt the feelings of another person—but only if he can help that person in the process. He will never hurt another person to make himself feel big.

I hope you will give some serious consideration in your discussion to this kind of man. You girls may want to compare him with James Bond and decide which one of these two people you would want to live with. You boys may want to compare him with Hugh Hefner who thinks so little of women that he dresses them as rabbits (he calls them bunnies) in his Playboy Clubs. You might want to think about what kind of person your wife will become if you treat her and if you treat all women in that way.

The beauty of a program like this is that you can discover for yourselves what men and women are like if you want to. It takes a lot of courage, but in the privacy of your classroom, honest communication is not as dangerous as it seems. Girls will tell you what they like in a boy if you sincerely ask them to and if you listen to and respect what they say. Even boys can be encouraged to talk about how they really feel if no one cuts them down or is sarcastic with them.

Mature discussion can't end in the classroom. I think that you have gathered by now that a very important part of my definition of manhood is that a boy has as few hang-ups as possible on women. If he feels in any way that women are inferior to him, if he is afraid of them, if he feels that they are sarcastic, hostile, or critical, he needs to get a lot closer to his own mother and learn to understand her better. This may be a tough process in some cases, but it's a necessary one.

Most girls, too, will want to carry their communications with men beyond the classroom and into their homes. If they feel that all men are overbearing, or bullying, or superior, or inferior, or in any other way vastly different from themselves, they are going to have to get much closer to their father. As they come to understand him better, they will begin to understand their own feelings toward men.

It's helpful if you realize that mothers and fathers are people, too. They have been faced with the same kind of training, background, and problems as you have. They are just as tired of being hurt and just as tired of playing "let's pretend" as you are. It is possible to talk to them and to understand them if you want to.

DISCUSS

You girls will want to be patient with the boys in starting this discussion. Some of them who are really interested in taking a look at themselves will probably be saying about now, "You sure know how to hurt a guy." Give them a little time to digest this whole idea of masculinity before you try to force them into the discussion.

Classroom Discussion. If you haven't already done so, it's time now to stop beating around the bush and start talking about the whole area of hurting and loving sex. You'll probably have to depend on the girls to start things rolling because girls are normally more open and honest about it. They don't have to pretend that they know all about it.

You girls—thousands of times you have told us in written questions how you feel about dates who are "all hands." *Say it out loud!* If you need a little extra motivation, remember next week we are going to be talking about "The Girl Matures." The boys will be picking on you, then. Girls—you have told us a thousand times how you feel about boys who brag about their conquests to other boys (and even lie about them) and what this does to your reputation. *Get it out and talk about it.*

What do you like in boys? Tell them. Boys—talk about your real feelings. Tell the girls what it's like to *be* a young man. Tell it like it is: the good things and the bad things.

All of this should start some interesting discussions, but it still won't be enough. No expert can tell you what needs to be talked about. Every boy is different and every girl is different. This time, *you* prepare the discussion. When you hit that slump, everyone in the classroom take out a piece of paper and write something on it so that no one is embarrassed. Elect someone for your discussion leader. Turn your suggestions into this leader. Then talk about them—all of them.

Come out of this discussion with a real understanding of what it means to be a man. You can learn to become free and open in your communications with the other sex if you want to, but you're going to have to talk. Nothing is going to happen if you hide.

Once again, be very careful about attacking people and hurting each other.

Discussion at Home. Have someone mimeograph all of the discussion topics that you put on paper. Take them home and show them to your parents. This should start discussion!

Chapter IV

The Girl Matures

OBSERVE

YOUR OBSERVATION OF WOMEN SHOULD BE ONE OF THE most interesting of them all. Look closely at the five you are observing. Since this chapter deals with maturity, you will want to be looking for some signs of maturity or immaturity. Treat each one individually:

1. *Self-confidence and self-respect.* Does she seem to be competent and capable? Does she take a great deal of pride in the fact that she is a woman? Or does she frequently complain about her state in life? If she does, are her complaints legitimate?

2. *Responsibility.* Is the woman you are observing honest with herself? Does she blame her husband and children for the problems that she faces?

3. *Her ideas of men.* Does she generally like most men, including her husband, or does she almost snarl when she talks about them?

4. *Demonstration of her femininity.* Does she assume the self-sacrificing role in the home and let everyone, including her children, walk over her? Does she attempt to dominate and control everyone around her? Is she

the "mother hen" type who is so concerned about her chicks that she is afraid to let them do anything on their own? Is she a selfish and self-centered person who is more concerned with how things appear than how they are? Or is she a person who likes herself and respects the people around her?

OBSERVE II

The girls around you are also searching for maturity. You can get some ideas of how well the three whom you are observing are succeeding by looking for the following things:

1. *Self-confidence.* You will want to look a little bit beyond what you see. Girls, like boys, often pretend a confidence they don't feel. The girl who is really self-confident is the one who is not afraid to question herself and who is honestly looking for some answers to her behavior.

2. *It would be surprising if any of the girls whom you are observing would be fairly mature in all areas.* Some girls seem reasonably confident in themselves in many ways, but have one or two areas in which they have no confidence at all. Why do you think that this is true?

3. *Honesty in talking about sex.* Do you think that the girls whom you know are more honest in talking about sex than the boys?

4. *Friendships.* Do friendships seem as important to the girls as they do to the boys? Does the word friend mean the same thing?

The mature woman plays it straight

Many sociologists have attempted to define femininity by observing women and discovering how they act. When they discover an action or trait that is fairly universal, they say that this trait is "feminine."

A lot of people are hurt by the words masculine and feminine. We talked in Chapter III about the boy who may seem to have a lot of feminine traits. His voice may be high-pitched; he may be much more interested in cooking than in becoming a charging linebacker. Yet, this young man may be far more masculine than the mass of muscles who sits across from him.

The same thing is true with girls. Many high school students are not much better than some older adults in the way that they judge femininity. Both women and men sometimes judge women by a series of physical measurements and the number of feminine games they know how to play. Just as men are judged by their ability to hurt other men, women are often judged by their physical beauty. This is very hard on the girl who is not particularly beautiful and who may be quite "masculine."

Just what should a woman be? If there is one thing that I am sure of, it is that no person living today can answer this question in any detail. No woman can become truly feminine until she becomes truly herself, and the structure of our society works against this. Like the boy, there are so many pressures on her to pretend to be something that she is not, that it sometimes becomes almost impossible for her to discover what she is. Also, like the boy, she has to discover peace of mind before she can achieve any degree of maturity. She has to know who she is and must like what she sees in herself.

This is why an honest discussion program presents such exciting possibilities. If you can get rid of your fears of exposing yourself to other people, you can get rid of the things about yourself that are phony and false and begin to come to grips with the real you. If the girl, for example, can discover within herself the courage to search for her real "you," this "you" will be feminine when she finds it—regardless of whether she is 6'4" or 5'2". She can help get rid of the false pressures that society puts upon her by taking a look at them, talking about them, and weighing them.

Puberty is again one of the most important events that shape the life of a girl. Before she can come to grips with herself and before men can hope to understand her, it is necessary to know, understand, and discuss just what happens to her during these short few years and how they affect her outlook for the rest of her life. We have no intention here of treating you to another detailed version of the biological changes that take place at this time. Most of you have been exposed to one or more excellent films on human reproduction that illustrate graphically and effectively exactly what happens to a girl's body during puberty. If you have not had an opportunity to view one of these films, any good audiovisual catalog will list several. For quicker information, any good biology book will explain the process thoroughly and completely.

We are much more concerned here with the effect that these changes have on the personality of the girl. Her physical changes have been described as a tremendous upheaval; it is far more violent than the comparable changes in a boy. Understanding them helps to explain why the average girl is more sensitive than the average boy, although even this is not necessarily true.

One part of the upheaval that every girl has to adjust to is menstruation. It will continue to influence her thinking and behavior from the time that she first matures physically until her change of life.

Menstruation, as you all know, is the passing of stored food in the form of blood from the uterus through the vagina. In this one short sentence are all kinds of worries and concerns that are difficult for the average man to understand. Yet it is important to the man who plans to marry some day to understand them, because they are going to be an important part of his life, too. We can only mention them briefly here in this chapter, yet we hope that you will discuss them thoroughly in your homes and in your classroom.

First of all, a vast number of women, and particularly teenage women, are faced with the question, "Am I normal?" They pick up a textbook and discover that the "normal" menstrual flow lasts approximately five days and occurs about every twenty-eight or thirty days.

We hope that in your class discussions you will come to know each other very well and understand that every human being is different, both physically and mentally, from every other human being. We hope that in the process, you will strike this word "normal" entirely out of the vocabulary that you use in dealing with people. There is no such thing as a normal human being. Some women have black hair, some have brown; some have green eyes, some have gray. Some flow for five days, some flow for nine. Some have a "regular" menstrual period and can almost set their watch by it; others never quite know when it is going to occur. If a woman is so irregular that she is concerned about it, she should, of course, talk with a doctor. A lot of simple medical aids are available today to help her become more regular.

Because of the tremendous upheaval that occurs in her body, a certain amount of tension always accompanies menstruation. But the degree of this tension varies a great deal because of the things that she has been taught about herself. Some mothers talked to their girls about the "curse," and they really meant it that way. They forbade their daughters to go swimming, horseback riding, and even walking. This built up a fear of menstruation that can literally make their daughters sick in bed for several days. Other mothers have treated it as just a fact of life and helped their girls to understand it and prepare for it. The important thing to keep in mind is that every husband and every wife are going to be faced with some irritation from premenstrual tension and menstrual tension. She may be sweet and loving when the man leaves her in the morning and something else again when he comes back to her at night.

Menstruation is also one of the signs associated with pregnancy in women. Most women stop menstruating when they become pregnant. This is again a simple statement that has a tremendous impact on all the people around her, as well as on herself. In marriage, it is one of the factors of her sexual maturity. If she feels loved, pregnancy may be a welcome and joyful event. But if she is not sure of her husband's love, fear of pregnancy can haunt her constantly.

The vast majority of the problems that young people have centering around sex and pregnancy would disappear quickly if only the people who love them could talk to them completely and honestly. Some of the high school principals warn their charges repeatedly about unmarried pregnancy, yet are not able to communicate the real reason for fearing it so much.

Some mothers, too, who thoroughly understand the destructive power of immature sexual relationships, don't know how to put their feelings into words. Instead, they hound their daughters, checking up on every monthly period. Since all of our bodies are controlled by the mind, this can create such tension on the daughter that she may actually skip periods or be late with her period. If she does not fully understand how pregnancy occurs, this can be really upsetting.

This kind of misunderstanding and failure of communications between teachers, parents, and children has another effect, too. It destroys the sense of trust that they have in each other and causes many young people to rebel. In the curiously illogical way we human beings have of doing things, the girl sometimes says to herself, "If that is all mother thinks of me, I am not worth very much anyway. Maybe that is the way I should be."

Yet it is not the daughter that the mother does not trust. It is herself; the way that she has taught her daughter about sexual things. She knows very well that she has not been able to talk with her daughter about all of the meanings of sex. Perhaps she has never discovered them herself. She wants to talk, but her own confusion in this area will not permit her to. She needs understanding and help from her daughter, not a rebellion that will destroy both of them.

Some mothers, too, are thoroughly confused by the fact that their daughters seem to change almost overnight from a nonsexual child to a sexual adult. Their confusion is certainly understandable. Many mothers do not even understand what happened to themselves during this period and how their feelings were related to the physical changes that were occurring within them.

Mothers are not alone in this. We have all been so cursed with misinformation that even those of us who deal with male and female sexuality every day do not even begin to understand female sexuality. This is not necessarily bad. In many ways, you are fortunate to be coming into the discussions without too much "knowledge"—the myths that even the experts have grown up with. We may have misinformed you. The knowledge of male and female sexuality that you gather through honest discussion may be more accurate—and it will have more meaning to you.

The "turned on" feeling that you young people talk

about is an example of an area that seems to be almost totally unexplored. We are going to talk about it here, and we will be offering some suggestions for your consideration. These suggestions have a certain validity since they are based on a lot of counseling and listening experience. Yet the examples that we use may not have any meaning to you except to help to start your discussion and eventually to arrive at some understanding of your feelings.

"Turned on" seems to mean different things to different people. Sometimes the definition seems to mean almost the same as "excited" or "good-feeling." A girl may say about a boy, "he turns me on," even though she has not had any contact with that boy. What she probably means is that he is an exciting person to be with or a nice person to talk to.

But young people use this expression in another way, too. They speak about being "turned on" completely, or "shook." This means that the body and the mind are completely sensitized to sex. A girl who is "shook" may breathe very deeply or quickly and may even feel a little faint. Her entire body is extremely sensitive to the touch. The vagina becomes wet and slippery, and a little of this wetness may be passed.

Getting "shook" or completely "turned on" is not very serious when we put it in perspective. What does it mean? It simply means that the girl is beautifully responsive. In marriage, she will want to be "shook" to perform the sex act with her husband. The ability to have this kind of feeling is good.

Yet counseling interviews indicate that this feeling

causes many girls all kinds of problems. They vary from girl to girl, of course. Some girls never experience it in dating at all, while some girls experience it often. This simply means that some girls are brought up in one way and some girls are brought up in another.

However, since the girl's feelings are so important to both her marriage and to her dating experiences, it is necessary that every girl take a look at how she does respond and arrive at some understanding of herself. Because so little is said in the literature about the responsiveness of women, we will be guessing a little as we describe the possible reasons why girls act as they do. Just as it is very unusual to have men talk about sexual impotency, it is also unusual for girls in our "hung-up" society to talk about lubrication of the vagina and the feelings that accompany it.

We can guess, though, that the girl who is unable to "turn on" at all grew up in a home in which sexual expression was completely repressed. She may never have seen her father kiss her mother and may have received few expressions of love from either of them. In other words, she may simply have never been taught to respond to love in any way.

This doesn't mean that the girl is frigid or cold. It merely means that she has a lot of mistaken notions about sex and love that she will have to do something about before she gets married. Her greatest problem now is worry and concern about herself. It can cause her to either draw into herself, or to experiment with sex to try to discover the response that she needs. Either one of these two approaches may hurt her a great deal. What she needs to do is to talk this thing through and to arrive at some understanding of why she feels as she does.

A girl who gets "shook" quite easily may have a similar problem with her background. She, too, may have parents who repressed their own sexuality and never knew how to give love to each other or to their children. However, this second girl may have reacted to the same kind of training in an entirely different way. She may have rebelled against it or rebelled against her parents. She may have thought about sex to the point where it has become an obsession for her and is on her mind almost constantly. Like the boy in our last chapter, the more she thinks about herself, the more guilty she becomes and the more frequently the "turned on" feeling occurs. With this girl, it can happen almost any time and in many different situations. Since she knows so little about herself, she may find her feelings very hard to control.

The third alternative is the one that most girls will want to work toward in their communications and their search for maturity. This is the ability to "turn on" when they are surrounded by love. Probably a great many more girls in today's society have this ability than in any previous generation. This girl has often had a great deal of love in her background. As a result, her response to love is spontaneous. Her body has been taught to respond to love through most of her growing-up years. When that "turned on" feeling happens to her, perhaps during her engagement to the man she intends to marry, she knows what it is and feels good about it. She has no sense of sin or wrong-doing because she actually has not done anything wrong; she is simply responding to love as God had intended her to respond. She has become a sexually mature person who is ready for marriage, and she knows it. In other words, she has achieved the same kind of maturity we spoke about in the boy: she is able to look at herself and like what she sees.

Nearly all parents love their children in the best way that they can. A few of them are able to communicate their love.

All of the problems of the girl have in some way been caused by her communications with other people. They are solved in the same way—through honest communications. Both the girl who cannot "turn on" at all and the girl who "turns on" too easily have never really been able to talk through their feelings about themselves and about sex. As soon as they do talk them through with other people, they experience a sense of relief and slowly their feelings begin to come back in balance. The best way to get rid of guilt and fear is to talk about it with other people who have many of the same feelings of guilt and fear.

I hope that in your discussions of the whole area of feminine sexuality, you will discard the word "normal" just as you did when you talked about menstruation. No woman is "normal" and we can be very glad that she is not. It is the infinite variety of the human being that makes life so interesting and challenging and makes it possible for the human race to accomplish so many things.

An example of this infinite variety is the experience of the girl with feminine masturbation. We can probably say (again, we are guessing, because we have no facts to back up this statement) that all girls, like all boys, have some experience with masturbation. This may range all the way from occasionally touching the breasts or clitoris and enjoying it, to playing with themselves often and feeling very guilty about it.

Feminine masturbation, like masculine masturbation, is far too complicated to simply write off as "sinful" or "introverting." It probably has a slightly different meaning to every girl who practices it. For example, feminine masturbation has a very practical place in quite a few of our modern marriages. It can be a loving thing. Some women may find themselves married to husbands who tend to be overstimulated sexually and who climax too soon. Since they want to love him and want to respond to him, they may use this method of preparing themselves.

For some girls, the response that they feel by touching themselves can be a reassuring thing. With other girls, it can lead to disgust and almost self-hatred.

Feminine masturbation, like masculine masturbation, only becomes a real problem when the girl's entire sexual background has made her feel guilty. Guilt focuses our minds on ourselves. Whenever we are constantly worried and concerned about ourselves, we are in trouble.

The girl who has been brought up to believe that any sexual pleasure at all is a sin for the single person is bound to have some problems any time that she touches herself, because she will quickly discover that this contact can be pleasant. She can get into the same kind of trap as the boy sometimes does by playing with herself, feeling very guilty about it, focusing her mind on it, which again leads to playing with herself and slowly toward withdrawal from other feminine society and eventually from both feminine and masculine society. Again, like the boy, she may search out other girls with the same kind of problem and even possibly become involved in feminine homosexuality, or lesbianism.

Probably, though, in our hung-up society, most young people of both sexes worry far too much about homosexuality. Every girl, like every boy, goes through a period when they have some very deep feelings toward friends of the same sex. This is simply a natural part of the process of learning to love. When we are talking about love and its real meaning, we are talking about our capacity to love everyone: not just people of the other sex. The feelings of some girls for their friend may go so deep that they may even "turn on" in a particularly emotional happening. They may feel real pleasure in the sexual feeling of closeness and want to hold each other at these times. They may enjoy walking hand in hand. This is a healthy sharing of feelings between girls and is exactly the opposite of the tendency toward lesbianism in which the person is thinking only of herself and her needs.

Regardless of which end of the love-sex pendulum the girl finds herself as she is going through this program, the kind of person that she will eventually become is entirely up to her. She can waste a lot of time criticizing parents, teachers, or other people who have caused her to have feelings of guilt. A more reasonable approach is to do something about these feelings.

People with healthy attitudes toward sex seldom have any problems with sex. Achieving a healthy sexuality is just as simple as taking out all of the things that go to make up you as a sexual person and looking at them frankly and honestly. Those feelings of guilt and sin are extremely damaging to the person, not only in marriage, but perhaps even more so before marriage. They lead to a hurting, destructive kind of sex. Perhaps even the word "lead" is not strong enough: They almost drive the young individual toward a hurting kind of sex.

In your observations, you will probably see many young people that this has happened to. Sex is on their mind constantly and yet they feel guilty about it and afraid of it. They have to resolve this conflict, so probably some night they have a beer party. Alcohol has a peculiar effect on the human personality. It tends to dissolve guilt and to heighten the sexual sensations. At the same time, it lowers the person's ability to have satisfying sexual relations. For young people who have tried to resolve their feelings about sex in booze, the results are seldom very pretty. They can only result in more hurt, more guilt, and more frustration.

Some of you have been very critical of your friends who have become involved in sexual escapades at beer and booze parties. You may want to take another look at your feelings about these people. You may want to listen to their boasting and bragging with a different kind of ear that is more sympathetic and recognizes the kind of hang-ups that lead to this kind of relationship. You can help them a great deal by giving them an opportunity to talk through their real feelings about

sex and about themselves, even if you first have to
listen to the boasting and bragging that they need to
do to cover up their real feelings.

Not everyone will be able to completely rid themselves of their sexual hang-ups in this classroom or
even in the conversations that they have with their
parents at home. With a few people who have extreme
problems of long duration, there is going to have to
be a counseling relationship with a mature person who
has a healthy respect for sexuality. Quite obviously, if
your sexual communications have been bad over a long
period of time, it is also going to take some time to get
rid of the bad things that you have learned. Just as
with the boys, the first person that a girl approaches
may not be able to help her. Yet, every girl who wants
to can find someone who can help if she tries.

One of the reasons that we spend so much time on
sexual communications in this book is that our attitudes toward sex have contributed so much toward our
mixed-up ideas about femininity and masculinity. The
Playboy idea of a woman is so prevalent in our society
that it shows up almost everywhere. Attractive women
have become sexual symbols. The idea seems to be that
a woman is so unimportant as a person that she is to
be used only for sex. Our advertisements on the T.V.,
radio, and in the magazines tell us that we need to
teach men to conquer women and to teach women to
relax and enjoy it.

This causes all kinds of problems with the girl who
is trying to grow up and mature and find herself as a
person. She is even taught to forget about becoming

a person and to first learn to play the sexual game. She is taught to be dishonest in many cases and not to express her real feelings. For example, society even makes it hard for her to tell a boy that she likes him or to ask him for a date. I hope that in your discussions you will start to think about a different kind of a girl: one with a real capacity to love. This girl loves herself because she has fully developed her talents and interests and knows who she is. She does not feel any need to play little games and pretend to be something that she is not. Like the mature man, she has a healthy respect for all other individuals of both sexes.

These are ideas and ideals. In closing this chapter, we would like to point out again that they are only openings toward healthy communications. We are not sure that open and honest communications are going to solve all human problems. We can be sure, however, that the pretending and phoniness and the hiding of ourselves in past generations has not worked very well. There is plenty of concrete evidence that human beings have never really explored love.

I hope that in your talks in the classroom and in the home you can stop being young men and young women with little games to play and start being people who talk to each other honestly about what kind of people you are.

DISCUSS

Classroom Discussion. In the last chapter we asked the girls to help the boys start the discussion. In this one, the boys will have an opportunity to ask the girls some questions. Boys ask a lot of questions when they can do so without other boys finding out about it. One of these questions is "Why do so many girls lead you on?" Now is the time to ask that question out loud. Young men and young ladies need to do a lot of talking about getting along together and understanding each other.

A lot can be accomplished if the girls in the classroom will talk about what it's like being a girl. There will probably be a great difference between how the boy sees the girl and how the girl sees herself. If anything is going to be accomplished, you're going to have to listen to each other very carefully.

I hope, too, that you will get into a thorough discussion on the whole meaning of femininity. A discussion of the chapter is a good starting point. Perhaps the girls can start by fully discussing the things that we've only guessed at in the chapter.

Discussion at Home. A very interesting thing to do will be to get both your father and mother talking about the meaning of femininity. In many cases, they haven't thought very much about it. Both of them thought that they "knew" what the word meant. Yet their definitions may have been very different.

As your parents become involved in this program, the things that you talk about in class will always be interesting to them.

Chapter V

A Complicated Me

OBSERVE

MOST OF YOU WILL HAVE ALREADY STARTED YOUR SELF-analysis. Now you can continue it by carefully watching the way the adults who are part of your observation group behave and the effect that their behavior has on the way their children act and believe. By watching other men and women and how they act toward their own children, you can come to have a lot of understanding about why you behave as you do, and what influences in your life cause you to behave in this way.

In some homes, you will see honesty being created; in some, dishonesty. Some fathers and mothers communicate responsibility to their children; some, irresponsibility. Most teach some form of love, but some teach hate.

You can learn about how the human personality is formed by simply watching the forming process. This doesn't require a great deal of knowledge about psychology. It does require watching what the wife does and how her husband reacts to it; watching what the husband does and how his wife reacts to it; finally, carefully observing how the children respond to both of them.

It doesn't make very much sense to get overly concerned about the things that you find in yourself by observing other people and by noting your own reactions to the people around you. It's much more important to discover what kind of person you are and then use that person in the most effective way possible. In this process, many of you will discover the source of your hang-ups. When you do, you will be able to handle them better. Careful observation is a major key to the intelligent discussion that will follow this chapter and to your eventual growth as a person.

OBSERVE II

The friends that you are observing will exhibit many different kinds of behavior. This behavior means that each of these people has had entirely different backgrounds and experiences. It will help you feel better about yourself to observe them closely and to understand that everyone has several areas of his personality that have not been developed adequately.

One of the things that you probably will quickly notice is that your friends need your companionship and understanding just as much as you need theirs. Many of us pretend that we don't need other people, but basically, we are all very lonely. One of the more amusing things that you will observe is how your friends test each other and test you. We are all afraid that if people discover what we are really like, they won't care for us anymore.

Facing up
to our feelings

Every human being often asks himself, "Why do I act as I do?" Many times a week each of us does something that is quite the opposite of what we want to do. Our reason may tell us to act in one direction, but very strangely, we act in another.

A typical example of this is a teenage boy or girl who wants very much to get along with his mother, yet feels somehow that they are drawing apart. He decides firmly that the next time they get into a conversation he will listen very carefully to what she has to say. He loves her and he knows that he loves her. Yet when she makes the smallest suggestion about his behavior, he finds himself almost shouting at her and he can't understand why.

Young adults are not a great deal different from old adults. Fear of mental illness occurs to all of us some of the time. It is a perfectly natural thing, when we are behaving in a way that we do not want to behave, to ask ourselves the question: "Am I cracking up or something?" This question doesn't become any easier to answer when we read the magazines, newspapers, and watch TV. There are all kinds of people who make an excellent living telling us how sick we all are and informing us of the mental strains that we all live under.

To illustrate how suggestion can work on a human

mind, you might think of a dangerous little game that most young people play or see played on their way to adulthood. In this game, Charlie Brown is "it"; he is the center of our attention. Charlie comes to school on this particular day feeling wonderful. What he doesn't know is that quite a few of his friends have decided that he is going to be sick. Charlie comes down the hall whistling until he meets Johnny. Johnny says to him, "What's the matter with you, Charlie? You look terrible." Charlie says, "What are you talking about? There is nothing the matter with me." But, Johnny shakes his head mournfully and walks away. A few minutes later he meets Sally, who is another one of his friends. Sally looks startled and says to Charlie, "For heaven's sakes, Charlie, why don't you go home?" Charlie is not so sure any more, so he says, "What do you mean? I feel fine." Sally tells him, "You're pale as a ghost. Are you sure you aren't running a fever?"

Charlie is not feeling as well as he did before. He remembers that his stomach didn't feel so good when he woke up this morning, but that he hadn't paid very much attention to it. Now it is really feeling queasy and uneasy, but he tells himself, "I'm not sick," and starts to whistle again—until he meets Bob.

Bob looks very concerned and drags him out of the hall and into the bathroom. He says, "Charlie, what are you doing in school?" Charlie says, "Why, what do you mean?" His stomach is churning rather violently by this time. Bob says to him, "You know darn well what I mean. It's fine to be a hero and come to school when you are half dead, but if you won't think of yourself, at least think of the other kids. Take care of yourself, man." And he slaps Charlie on the back.

By now Charlie feels terrible. He can't make it out of the bathroom for awhile. Finally, he staggers down to the principal's office and gets a permission slip to go home. His mother is somewhat surprised, but writes it off as a bug. The doctor shakes his head and says, "These kids are certainly under a lot of tension in school today." Meanwhile, good old healthy Charlie wonders whether he will survive.

I am certain that you have all seen a lot of examples of sickness induced through autosuggestion. Around every school there are all kinds of amateur psychiatrists who find problems almost everywhere and are always willing to "help" you with these problems. Many times they create more problems than they solve. Certainly the young adult will want to face the whole area of mental health realistically and try to begin to understand why he acts as he does.

The statistics on mental illness that we are constantly hearing about are like all statistics—they can be very deceiving. If we are talking about people who are really mentally ill, who are what the helping professions like to term psychotic, we are probably talking about one person in every 1,000—or perhaps even a smaller number than this. Even this small percentage has probably been helped toward mental disturbance as much by the fact that they are very afraid of mental illness and constantly thinking about their "odd" behavior as by any other one factor. The human personality has a tremendous capacity for believing in itself, and if other people would concentrate on letting our emotions alone, we probably could work out most of our problems by ourselves.

The psychotic, then, is a very rare bird who completely detaches himself from reality. But what about the neurotic—the other scare word of mental illness?

There are all kinds of definitions for the word neurotic, but we can probably boil down our definition of a neurotic to this: "A neurotic personality is one that is in conflict with itself or is in conflict with society." Under a definition of this kind, all that we can possibly say to you is, "Hello, fellow neurotics." All of us fit that definition. There is no such thing as a person who is not in conflict with himself and with a great deal of society.

What I am suggesting here for your consideration is that it is perfectly "normal" to be neurotic. The human being is far from being a perfect machine. All of us have very strong feelings in some directions that seem unreasonable to other people, and sometimes even may seem unreasonable to ourselves.

In talking with your parents about mental stability, I often say that the normal human being is a person who has most of his mental screws screwed down tight, but has a half dozen or so that are loose. The problem with most of us is that we spend so much time worrying about the loose ones and ignoring the tight ones that quite a few of them loosen in the process.

What I am saying here is that it is not only normal to be neurotic; it is good. The world's work is done by people who have conflicts. They have a driving urge to do a particular thing that needs to be done. When I think of the completely adjusted person who has no strong and compulsive inner drives, I think of a herd of sheep patiently following a shepherd. Not much is ever done by sheep. ·

I would like to suggest a more reasonable definition of a well-adjusted person: He or she is an individual who has many strong and seemingly unreasonable conflicts with both society and himself raging within him, but in the process of maturing, he has come to realize *why* he has these conflicts and *how* they can be channeled in useful, constructive directions.

Becoming an adult certainly does not mean that you become a nonentity—a person who has all of his drives and feelings and passions under full control all of the time. If this were the definition of an adult, this would be rather a sad world and a dull one.

There are almost as many definitions for the words "maturity" and "adult" as there are authors trying to define these words. Many of these definitions attempt to include age as a part of the definition. I think that you already have looked at enough so-called adults to realize that age doesn't have very much to do with it. All of us know a great many middle-aged children, and some of us know mature people who are quite young.

There seems to be only one universal characteristic of maturity: *A mature adult is a person who accepts responsibility for his or her own acts.* In other words, an adult does many of the same foolish things that children do but shows his maturity by saying, "This is my act; I am responsible for it." As part of this responsibility, the mature person has looked deep within himself and has some understanding of why he acts as he does.

Probably this was not as difficult in the "good old days" as it is today. Then society was quite simple and definitions were simple. Nearly every boy knew, for example, that he was "just like his old man, or just the opposite of his old man." But today, these definitions have been complicated by a wealth of psychological theories. The business of self-evaluation is associated with technical jargon like Oedipal complex, castration anxiety, and many more. Most of us feel that we need a lot of special knowledge to even begin to come to grips with ourselves.

While it is true that the human being is extremely complex, it is also true that nearly everyone can learn to understand himself quite well and, as a result, to operate effectively most of the time. If he is willing to think back honestly about the way he was reared and the kinds of people he came into contact with, he will come to know himself better. In a very real sense the human being is a composite of all of the things that have happened to him and of all of the contacts that he has had with people, plus the things that he has added himself through the thinking and reasoning process.

Ancient philosophers tried to divide the person into two parts: the body, and the mind or soul. It is not as simple as that, but let's follow this ancient plan for a little while to get some idea of the forces that help us to finally arrive at the answer to the question, "Why do we act as we do?"

It helps me to think of myself as a whole person with two parts that are constantly influencing each other. To make it very simple, I call these the *thinking parts* and the *feeling parts*.

The feeling part of us is an organic thing. In other words, it has to do with our body and especially with our glands and nerves. The way that they respond to any given situation gives us our "feeling" about that situation. Their reaction is automatic, but most reactions of glands and nerves are not instinctive. They have actually been taught how to respond to certain situations by the unique experiences that we all have in growing up. Our bodies have been *conditioned*. What we mean by that is that our glands and nerves have been trained from infancy to act in a particular way.

To illustrate how this conditioning works, we might use a puppy as an example. This puppy belongs to a mean little kid who is always pulling the puppy's tail, kicking at him, and slapping him. You have all seen what happens to this puppy whenever someone moves a hand or a foot very quickly in his direction—he cowers and cringes.

Now something strange happens to the puppy. The neighbor kid trades him to a good little kid who really loves puppies. He is kind and gentle to him always, and the puppy relaxes and begins to enjoy life a little more. As the puppy grows to a dog he has good treatment. One day the good little boy makes a fast move in the puppy's direction with his hand as if he were going to slap him. What happens in spite of the good treatment that this dog has from his new master? He still cowers and cringes. His glands and nerves have been taught that "when someone moves his hand fast in your direction, you are going to get hit and it hurts, so duck." This is what he does.

But the glands are conditioned in a good sense, too. You have probably all seen the dog who has had good handling when he was small and has complete trust in humans. He has some pretty terrible experiences when he becomes a stray, because whenever he sees a human being he gets a good feeling and wants to go over and be petted. Even after he gets kicked off the porch a half dozen times, he still comes back to be friendly with humans.

We are not puppies, of course. Yet the feeling part of us reacts in the same way. The conditioning of the body starts at home shortly after birth. This is easy to see. The human being at birth has almost no personality at all, so it gathers in experiences during the first few years of its life. We can compare it to an empty sack at birth: each contact that it has with a thing or a person is a brand new experience for it, so conditioning factors pour into this empty sack like sand from a shovel. As the infant grows and matures, the personality begins to fill and the top of the sack slowly closes. Finally, the new experiences can only come through the side of the sack which has a tough, but porous membrane. In other words, most experiences are already repetitions of experiences that have happened before, and unless they are different, they simply bounce off the personality and do not penetrate it. If they are strong enough, or persistent enough, they will replace the elements of personality that are already in the sack. But, only experiences that are very strong or very different or are continued for a long time will really penetrate the membrane and displace the elements that are already there.

This is why the one person who most affects the child's formation is the mother. She is the one who is with the child almost constantly when his "personality sack" is almost empty, so she is the individual who provides most of his initial conditioning experiences. The instant the child is born, the mother, or some person who acts as the mother, starts training the feeling part of the infant to respond to a certain situation in a given way.

One of the first things that the mother teaches the infant is that mother is "good" or mother is "bad." When she holds him very lovingly against her breast, she is teaching his glands and nerves to make him feel good toward her, and, in a sense, to feel good toward all women.

Mother, of course, is not always "good." Because she is a human being, sometimes she is "bad." She is subjected to all of the other problems of every other human being. She has colds, flu, hates to get up at night, is treated like a dog or a princess by her husband, and probably can't stand the sound of a child screaming. So ordinarily the feeling part of the child is taught that mother is a mixture of bad and good. When she acts in a certain way, her actions teach us to laugh and smile. When she acts in another way, our nerves and glands learn to duck.

The infant has the same kind of relationship with father, although perhaps not as close. Father again teaches the feeling part of us how to respond to him, and again in a sense, how to respond to all men.

By the time we are ready to start school, we have accumulated all kinds of very strong feelings about many things that happened around the home. The feeling part of us tells us, for example, that mealtime is a comfortable time—or that mealtime is a terrible time; and these feelings will influence how we feel about food all of our lives. If mother is a good listener, the feeling part of us will tell us that "you can talk to women." If dad is irritable and grouchy most of the time, he will have taught us "don't try to talk to men." These feelings are strong and they are not easily changed, because they are a part of the things that our body has been taught for six years or more.

By this time change comes only through the forceful experience that bursts through the protective membrane that we have built around us or through repeated experiences that are different from, or in conflict with, those that our personality has already experienced. An example of this is the change that occurred in the feeling part of me after the age of 40. During the growing up years, one of the occupations that really intrigued me was bus driving. I felt that when I became an adult I wanted to drive one of those big buses. I read everything I could about the career of bus driving and learned that these men are among the most competent drivers in the world, highly trained, highly skilled, and have an excellent non-accident rate. My feelings toward Greyhound bus drivers, of course, were very good; it gave me an extremely pleasant feeling all through my life simply to be on a bus.

Several years ago we were returning from a neighboring city late at night and in a snowstorm. Visibility was almost zero. In passing us, the luggage door of a bus flew open and struck the side of our car. The last thing that Jeanette and I saw as we went into the ditch was this huge bus bearing down on us. Since that time, the thinking part of me has told the feeling part of me over and over again that there is no reason to be afraid of Greyhound buses. I have told myself hundreds of times that these are some of the best drivers on the road and that the chances of having an accident with a bus are one in a million.

But all of this talking doesn't change the feeling part of me very much. When I look in my rearview mirror and see a huge bus coming up behind me, the palms of my hands begin to sweat and I visibly cringe and tighten my grip on the wheel. If it happens to be snowing, it is a real temptation to get clear off the road. My glands and nerves are still "seeing" that big bus bearing down on us and are still doing what that bus taught them to do on the night of our accident.

There are, of course, many experiences that change our personalities in life that are not so dramatic. A child whose mother is extremely critical, and who has taught his personality to fear women and to be silent when he is around them, may find a female teacher who takes a great deal of interest in him in school. When she first tries to relate to him, of course, he will be suspicious and tend to withdraw. But as his experiences with her continue to be good, the way that he feels about women in general will slowly change and he will become more comfortable with them.

In most cases, the small child has no real conflict or problems with his feelings. They are either bad or good, and generally he accepts them in this way. It is only as he gets older and the thinking part of him becomes more active that real problems develop.

What you often hear described as a neurosis is really a conflict between what we think and what we feel. It may also be a conflict between two different kinds of feelings. Every one of us has a lot of these conflicts simply because we all deal with human beings, and no human being is ever consistent enough to act toward us in one way only.

Race prejudice is an excellent example of a conflict that exists in nearly everyone, white and black, who has any education or who is doing any thinking. It is almost impossible to conceive of anyone 25 years old or more whose feeling part is not prejudiced. The feeling part of white society has been conditioned to think of Negroes in terms of low intelligence, comic entertainers, or porters, and perhaps dangerous and unreliable as well. This is conditioned fear; the one that was expressed in the song from *South Pacific*, "You Gotta Be Taught To Hate." As we become older, our mind tells us that the feeling part of our reaction toward Negroes is wrong. So now we have a conflict. Our mind tells us that Negroes are just people and that we can't put them all into a nice neat little mold. But the feeling part of us continues to make us uncomfortable and fearful of them.

As a person who regards himself as intelligent and Christian, I have found it extremely difficult to accept the fact that I am prejudiced. Intellectually, I believe wholeheartedly in the equality of the races in every sense of the term, and would have absolutely denied that I was prejudiced. It was a very rude awakening when I began to come in personal contact with many Negro males. With white people, I have likes and dislikes, and if I don't like them or don't believe what they say, I feel perfectly free to ignore them or tell them about it. With the Negro, however, I am like Avis—I try harder. Because I am fighting the feeling part of me, I would not think about telling a Negro, for example, that I don't particularly like company in the morning. If one came to my table at breakfast, I would feel compelled to put down my newspaper and talk to him. This feeling kind of prejudice must be common to all of us, both white and black. The black man who regards himself as unprejudiced probably also feels the need to try harder to overcome his feeling about whites. Perhaps the only person who has no conflict is the real bigot—the person whose mind and feelings both agree that black people are no good or white people are no good. According to the way some psychiatrists define a neurosis, these people should be well adjusted simply because they are not in conflict with themselves.

The sexual conflicts that we all develop in some way as we go through puberty are an example of a conflict between more than one kind of feeling. The initial contacts that we have with each other at this point teach the feeling part of us that sex is good. Yet many of the experiences that we have had with parents and teachers have taught our emotions that sex is bad. A dozen different and conflicting ideas concerning the whole idea of sex and sexuality are thrown at us to further confuse the thinking part of us. It is little wonder, then, that young adults spend so much time being concerned about themselves as sexual persons. Again, it is little wonder that the minds and emotions of some young adults are focused so strongly on sex that responsible sexual behavior becomes a real chore for them.

Understanding why we act as we do, then, becomes a continuing process of looking back at the important things that have happened to us through our lifetimes, and on how these things might have influenced our behavior. Most of the things we do that seem unreasonable to us can be traced quite easily to our conditioning and training in the home. When we shout at mother, for example, it doesn't mean that we are mean and that we hate our mother; it simply means that the feeling part of us is angry at her for something that she has done. In a sense, mother has trained the feeling part of us to be angry at her. When we want desperately to ask a particular girl for a date, sometimes we find ourselves unable to do so. Probably it is simply the feeling part of us saying, "It is really no use talking to this girl; women never listen anyway"—again, something that the feeling part of us has learned from mother or perhaps an older sister.

What has all this to do with how we act now? It has almost everything to do with explaining our behavior to ourselves. A girl, for example, may have a feeling that all boys are on the make, or that no man can be trusted—even though the thinking part of her recognizes that a lot of boys are responsible and trustworthy.

Some boys have developed a hurting kind of relationship with girls. They criticize them, run them down, look down on them. Even though they see some girls who deserve and earn the respect that every man should give a woman, their early experiences "tell" them to behave in an immature way.

The feeling part of us doesn't change very easily. All of our lives all of us have so-called neurotic conflicts between what we know to be true and how we feel. Many times the feeling part of us is temporarily in control, and out of habit we do some things that we feel are stupid. Unless we understand why we have acted in this way, we can really feel guilty and sometimes even hate ourselves.

Once we can honestly face what our feelings really are, it becomes much easier to handle them and channel them in the right direction. Anger is a good example. A lot of people spend most of their lives trying to suppress feelings of anger because they feel that anger is always bad. Nothing can be further from the truth. Once we have located and faced the people who have built into us the feelings of anger, we can channel these feelings and redirect them toward things that we need to be angry about.

When we locate the source of the feelings that to us are unreasonable, there are many ways of handling them. But first it is necessary to admit that they exist. A good example of the entrance of feelings into our everyday life is the current ecumenical meetings that take place between members of various religions. Nearly every Catholic of the older generation was conditioned by his parents and teachers to fear and sometimes even to hate members of the Protestant religions. Methodists were just as strongly conditioned toward Lutherans. Nearly all Christians were conditioned to be suspicious of each other. Today, every thinking person knows that these feelings are nonsense—that the members of every religion are people and that most of them are sincere.

Yet, when we meet at any sort of interfaith gathering, the old prejudicial feeling part of us is still at work. If we know this and admit this—and especially if we admit this to each other—these feelings become much more easy to handle. We can sit down honestly and say to each other, "It is not very easy for us to change the way we feel, but we certainly can change what we do." On the other hand, if we try to suppress these feelings and pretend that they don't exist, we can depend on them to literally burst right out of us and destroy everything that we have tried to do. We are not being honest with ourselves. Feelings cannot be suppressed; they can only be recognized and controlled.

When we talk about this, a lot of people say to us, "This doesn't help very much; the feelings just don't go away." Many people, for example, feel very guilty when they are around their father. They are tense and tight and sometimes feel almost a hatred for him. There is a real conflict between how they feel and the idea that everyone has to love father.

If there is one part of the message of Christianity that is clear, it is that we are *not* responsible for how we feel. We *are* responsible for what we do with these feelings. In His life, Christ pointed out very forcefully that it isn't enough to love someone who loves us, but that we need to learn to love those who hate us or whom we hate. But we can't begin to love until we know and admit our real feelings.

Most feelings can be changed once we have discovered why we have them. But generally, it is a very long process of substituting good experiences for bad experiences until finally the personality feels comfortable with the things that we had formerly detested.

However, a very large part of maturing and growing up is accepting ourselves as we are and recognizing that there are some feelings that are simply too deep-rooted or that have persisted too long to change. These we need to recognize, learn to laugh at, and in some extreme cases, even stay away from. In this way, it becomes possible for most of us to act in a way that we want to act—most of the time. It also permits us to assume responsibility for our own acts—most of the time. This is maturity.

DISCUSS

Probably no one in the class is going to want to get into an immediate discussion of himself. An excellent

PROPERTY OF ST. CYRILS CHURCH
BANNISTER, MICHIGAN

place to start is by talking about the people you have observed. The chapter that you have just read is certainly not the final word on character formation. Everybody's personality is formed in a different way from everyone else's. Your ideas on how your personality is formed are just as valid as anyone else's. They are probably more valid, in fact, since they apply more directly to you.

Your discussion will start fast if you tell each other about things that you have observed in homes and compare your ideas with how these things have influenced the formation of the personalities of the children. As a help in starting your discussion, here are a few specific points that you may want to talk about:

1. How did the parents that you observed create confidence in each other? In their children?

2. Did any of them destroy the child's confidence in himself? How did they do this?

3. All of the friends that you have observed tend to be moody at times. But some are much more moody than others. Why do you think they are this way?

4. When the parent is very domineering, what effects do you notice in the child? Does the domineering parent perhaps have a different effect on different children in the family?

5. Did the homes that you observed help the children in them to learn to make their own decisions? To accept responsibility for these decisions? How did the parents accomplish these things?

6. Did the homes that you observed teach real love to their children? Did some of them force their chil-

dren to search for love someplace else? Do the teachers in your school teach love? How do they do this?

Perhaps now you will want to start talking about
yourselves. You can help each other if you can express
your feelings about another person honestly. If you are
being critical of that person, though, make certain that
you are pointing to only one characteristic that you
don't like or one particular thing that you think that
he should face. You can't help anyone to change from
what he is unless he also feels that you care for him.

Go as far as you like with this discussion. Don't be
afraid of it. Some of the things that you may hear about
yourself from other students or from the teacher, or
that the teacher may hear about herself (or himself)
from the students might hurt a little bit. But the small
hurts that you experience in honest communications
are far better than the deep hurts that always result
from trying to hide from yourself. The time to straighten
out your feelings and attitudes is *now*. You are still very
close to the source of them and you haven't formed the
destructive habits that most adults have of hiding and
covering these feelings even from themselves.

Discussion at Home

Parents are people who are very much aware of the
fact that they've made a lot of mistakes in rearing you.
Just like all people, they sometimes try to cover up
these mistakes and hide from them and insist that they
were right. It isn't going to help your communications
if you go home and suddenly say, "Pa, you were 'all
wet' in the way that you raised me." Whenever you

attack a person, he has a tendency to defend himself. A much better way is simply to tell your parents again about the discussions in the school. Then, if there is something that is particularly "bugging" you, tell your parents about it and explain that you would like to talk it over. Don't waste your time or theirs in blaming them or in blaming yourself. Development of your full capacity as a human being and as a person is far too important to waste time on regrets. Besides, in most cases, no one has been to blame. Until you start being honest with each other, all of you will make a lot of mistakes in your human relations. Your parents, too, are a product of their environment and training. Like you, they have probably done the best job that they knew how to do with the equipment that they had to work with. Make sure that they know that you care for them when you are discussing things that are important to both of you.

Chapter VI

Communications Now and in Marriage

OBSERVE

GOOD COMMUNICATION IS AN ART THAT HAS BEEN SO
badly neglected in many homes and in most schools
that you will probably want to read the chapter first
this time, as a background and basis for your observations. You have already discovered that it is not easy
to communicate openly and honestly with the other
people in your classroom, with your parents, and with
your teachers. But I hope that you have also discovered by now that it does become much easier as you
practice it.

In your observation of the five married couples that
you have selected, you will again try to get the feel
of the kind of communications that take place in these
homes and what effect these communications have on
the total relationship of both the parents and their children. Make your observations as carefully and accu-
rately as possible. Please do not be too quick to say,
"This couple communicates well," or "This couple communicates poorly." Regardless of how well or how
poorly the couple whom you observed communicates,

all of them can stand some improvement. If you are going to help your own communications, it is going to be necessary for you to carefully observe and analyze the things that make communications work and the things that make communications break down.

The suggested list of observations for this chapter is a little longer than some of the others. The reason for this should already be obvious. The way that you talk to people and relate to people is going to largely decide how you get along with them and how much you like yourself. Here are some of the things you will want to look for:

1. In the homes that you are observing, do the man and woman both communicate equally well? Does one tend to talk too much and the other talk too little? Why do you suppose that this is?

2. Have the couples that you are observing developed mechanisms for escaping open and honest communications? Here are some of the ways that people avoid each other and avoid talking about things that have to be settled between them: a) Constant TV watching. b) Either the man or the woman is out of the home almost every evening. c) When they are together, they feel that they have to be "doing something," rather than just sitting and talking and enjoying each other's company. d) Is one or the other member of the family constantly buried in a book or in a magazine? e) Does the woman seem to save all her housework until the man is home in the evening

so that she can be busy in another room? f) Is the dinner table a place where the family talks freely about everything, or is it a place in which there is an attitude of "shut up and eat"? g) Is the man constantly taking trips alone, or is the woman so busily involved in "doing good things" for the church or community that she has little time to get acquainted with her family at home? h) Is the man in the household spending many evenings on his job? Is he really that busy, or is he avoiding communications?

We are all afraid of honest and open communications. Perhaps you will notice many other ways that husbands and wives avoid talking about things that really matter in the home.

3. Does one or the other of the parties nag a great deal?

4. Is one or the other of the parties very sarcastic?

5. Do the couples listen carefully to each other?

6. Are they constantly talking about inconsequential things like the latest TV program, the football game, or gossiping about other people?

7. Is there a great deal of tension in the home when the man and woman are in the room together? When they are talking to you or some other person, do they join in the conversation together, or do they seem to compete with each other?

8. Does either the man or the woman do a great deal of pretending? Does one or the other act superior and indicate by his attitude that he has all the answers?

9. Can they get honestly angry with each other with-

out feeling that the slightest disagreement is going to destroy their marriage? Are they "walking on eggs" whenever they're around each other?

OBSERVE II

Your friends have many of the same problems with communications that their parents do. In addition to the above, many of which you will also observe in your friends, you may want to watch for some of these signs of insecurity in their communications with others:

1. Do they tend to imagine that their friends are angry with them when they really are not? Is this because they have not talked things over sufficiently to "clear the air"?

2. Are they reluctant to talk about themselves and their feelings?

3. Aren't most of the problems that occur between friends largely misunderstandings that can easily be cleared up by talking them over?

The basis of communication is love

In the last chapter we talked about the many things that form the personality of the individual. In this one we will be talking about communications, the most important tool for building personality now and building happiness in marriage later.

Probably we should start with a working definition of communications. It means a lot of things to a lot of people and there are all kinds of communications. But in this chapter we will be concerned with a special meaning. Let us simply define communications as "talking about things that really matter."

You have already discovered that this definition encompasses some of the greatest problems of the human being. By this time in life, one or the other of your parents has probably become a little hard to talk to. A certain teacher—everyone has a teacher like this—simply doesn't understand you. Many times communications look hopeless, and it seems much easier to talk about things that aren't important at all. In that way, no one gets hurt.

But that is not as easy as it sounds. We really get hurt when we don't communicate. You may have already discovered this with a close personal friend. What happens when you assume that this friend knows what you are thinking? If you have had any experiences at all with friendships, you know the hurts that can develop through misunderstanding. They could have been very simply cleared up through the loving kind of communication—talking things over with a person that you care for.

Communications is just another area of life in which answers don't come easy. In our office we have a standing joke that goes like this: "This office is a place where everyone talks about communications, but no one communicates." The purpose of this joke is to keep us all aware of the great misunderstandings that always occur when we get into a pattern of thinking that says "if they really cared for us, they would know how we feel without our telling them."

One of the most significant symbols of my life is a little sign that you see on many executive's desks. It simply says "the buck stops here." Probably this is the most important message of this book; "the buck stops here" with you. It is very comfortable sometimes to believe that we are not responsible for our own behavior; that we are simply a creature of our training and background. I like to think of the human being as something a great deal more than just a conglomeration of all of the things that other people injected into him on his path toward maturity. We are responsible for all our own behavior, and until we accept that responsibility, life has no meaning or enjoyment.

Responsible behavior comes through self-respect. It is the opposite of selfishness. Selfish people are simply people who have never learned to communicate with themselves. They don't understand why they act as they do because they have never been able to face themselves honestly. They have been grabbing for things and for love, somehow trying to fill a personality that has no confidence in itself from outside rather than from inside. Talking to yourself realistically about yourself becomes the most important thing you can do. Until you come to an understanding and accept what you are, you will have nothing at all to give to other people. Since communication is your most important tool in your own self-analysis, we would suggest that you begin by taking a look at your talking skills.

Probably all of you will fall into one of three basic types of communicators. If you look around you and observe the people with whom you associate, all of these types and combinations of these types will be very easy to recognize.

1. *The Strong, Silent Type*

Sometimes this person is your best friend, and sometimes he is you. This person never seems to get too involved in conversations and only really talks when he is in an area in which he feels completely confident. We make up all kinds of myths about this person and sometimes we really believe that he is the strong, silent type who depends on himself, who doesn't need other people. But is he?

The silent type kids himself by saying, "I don't need to talk. Talking just gets me in trouble. I can depend on myself." Yet, if he were honest, he would tell you of the tremendous feeling of loneliness that he has at times and the real sense of being apart from people simply because he feels that he can't communicate with them.

The silent person, of course, has a reason for his feelings about talking. He has been hurt by communications through his growing up years. Somewhere along the line the feeling part of him has been taught, "It is no use talking to people; nobody listens anyway."

Sometimes his experiences in talking with people are even more drastic than this. Perhaps he has been criticized for the things he has said or even severely punished when he tried to talk with someone about something that was important to him. Every time that this happened, the feeling part of him "learned" the hard way that, "It just doesn't pay to talk; you get clobbered if you do."

The strong, silent type faces many problems in his relations with people. Perhaps the most important one is the feeling that people don't understand him. This is not just something that he thinks; it is true. People are important to all of us, and we have a great deal of curiosity about them. When they don't—or aren't able —to tell us who they are, our imagination immediately goes to work and we build up false ideas about them. Very often we like the silent person, but do we really understand him? Isn't it very frustrating at times trying to figure out what kind of person he is and especially what he really thinks about us?

Most often a noncommunicator doesn't like himself very well. Every single school day is something of a struggle with him. Something may come up in class that is interesting. He would like to participate, but somehow he can't bring himself to do it. On dates and parties, he often finds himself alone in a corner wishing that he could join the fun but not knowing how to go about it. He pretends that he is bored or not interested, but the real him stands there hurt and alone.

Because he has trouble giving very much of himself to other people, very often he doesn't get very much in return. For example, he (or she) probably doesn't get as much attention from teachers, friends, or parents, as he would like. When he does get attention, it is often angry attention. We are all frustrated when we cannot talk to people and we tend to take our feelings out on the silent person. He is the one who frustrates us. Each time this happens, the feeling part of the silent person gets hurt again, and each time it becomes a little harder for him to talk with people.

The people of your own age can sometimes really be hard on a person who finds it hard to talk. How many "snobs" do you have in your school? Are they really snobs? Or are they people who have a great deal of trouble talking to other people? Do they really feel that they are better than you are, or are they simply afraid to talk to you?

Since the strong, silent type is only one kind of personality, the things that happen to him are certainly not all bad. A lot of people like him because he may appear to be a good listener and most of us like to talk and be heard. Very often, without realizing it, he tends to chum and even date a person with almost exactly the

same type of communication problem, but who ex-
presses it in an entirely different way. This is a second
type that most of you will recognize.

2. *The Compulsive Talker*

Nearly every junior or senior class, and a huge percentage of marriages, has one of these types who seem
to be talking most of the time. He (or she) has a com-
ment to make about everything. Again we tend to build
up myths about the compulsive talker. The silent person may say to himself, for example, "I wish I could
be like him; he can talk to anyone."

Yet, if we examine this "easy talker," we will find
out quickly that communicating may not be coming
so easily for him after all. He shares many of the same
communication problems with the noncommunicator.
During his growing up years, he probably had a great
deal of trouble being understood by one or the other
of his parents and felt it necessary to repeat things over
and over to make himself understood. This is why he
feels it necessary to overcommunicate. In a sense, the
feeling part of him is saying, "If I just say this often
enough to enough people, perhaps they will begin to
understand me and like me."

The overcommunicator faces some problems in his
contact with other people, too. Some people feel that
he is a bore because he is constantly repeating himself.
Other people feel that he has a real need for attention
and is trying to get "brownie points" by always talking
in class. A lot of people have told him in one way or
another to "shut up." However, he *cannot* shut up that

easily. He feels that no one will understand him if he does. Like the silent person, he too, feels very insecure at times. We all do.

There are some benefits, too, in being a compulsive talker. Many people like him. Quite often, he is the "life of the party," and is envied by people whose communication problem is more apparent.

Sometimes we say about the compulsive talker, "If he'd just shut up once in a while, he'd be a nice guy." About the silent type we say, "If he'd just let you know what he's thinking, he'd be a nice guy." When we put these two ideas together, we approach the third type of talker.

3. *The Balanced Communicator*

Here we are *really* talking about a mythical figure; a person who simply does not exist in real life. But this is an ideal that we are all striving for and one that all of us are going to have to approach if we ever hope to mature in our relations with ourselves and with other people. In your class, you may have many people who are already approaching this kind of relationship in quite a few different areas.

I think we all should take a look at this ideal, not only as we are going through this self-evaluation program, but all through our life. Here are some of the characteristics of the good communicator:

a. *The balanced communicator is open.* This simply means that he is willing to talk about anything that is important. He doesn't feel any need at all to express his opinion on something that he doesn't know anything about.

b. *The balanced communicator is honest.* The name of the game that most of us play all of our life is "Let's Pretend." "Let's pretend" that we are something that we are not. We are continually trying to put ourselves in a better light with the people around us—our wives, husbands, friends, and even our children. All of us play this little game sometimes; we are all a little phony. We only mature when we learn to be honest with and about ourselves—most of the time.

We all play another little game that is perhaps even more objectionable. The name of this game is "Let's Blame John." There is a scientific name for it—projection. What it simply means is that we refuse to accept responsibility for our own acts; instead we tend to blame these acts on other people. It is when you flunk a test and then say, "My kid brother had the television on all last night. Wait until I get home." Obviously, it is really not the kid brother's fault; you could have gone down in the basement, up in the attic, or even over to some other person's house if you really intended to study.

Projection is when you are thinking of a girlfriend and pull out into the street without looking—then you swear at the other fellow who narrowly missed you. It is when you tear up to your room in a temper with Mother because "She doesn't understand me"—although you have not done anything at all to help her understand you.

In other words, projection is something that you did

—today—perhaps many times—simply because you are human. Everyone in this program can take a quick look at himself and think of all the times when he blamed other people for things that were really his fault. Yet, projection is one of the things that the good communicator has to learn to handle if he hopes to mature. Someplace along the line, he has to learn to say to himself—most of the time—"This is my act. I am responsible for it."

c. *The balanced communicator knows himself,* and generally he likes himself. He isn't afraid to take a hard look at himself and try to discover why he acts as he does. He has reached the kind of maturity in which most of his communications with other people are real, honest communications and, as a result, he feels fairly confident with Number One.

d. *The balanced communicator is a good listener.* This is a tricky area because all of us like to feel that we are good listeners. It means that when he is listening to others, he is listening carefully and thinking about what is being said, rather than how it affects him. It means that he listens to learn, rather than listening impatiently until he can get in his "2¢ worth."

Marriage is not much different than any other kind of life. The greatest difference, perhaps, is that your experiences in living together 24 hours a day are much more highly concentrated. Intelligent, learning listening is one of the real keys to a successful marriage—just as it is one of the keys to just plain successful living.

When we are the topic of conversation, nearly all of us listen defensively. When someone is talking to us about *us*, do we always listen to learn? Or are we listening instead to pick up the mistakes in what they are saying and to gather ammunition to strike back at them?

Very few of us listen to other people intelligently and none of us listen to other people intelligently at all times. We tune people out when they are saying things we don't like to hear. Every one of us has a great many areas in which we listen defensively and hear only those parts that we want to hear. An example of this is the way that many people in our country listen to what the Negroes are saying. Basically, the message that is screaming from the ghettos is: "We want an even break with Whitey." But what is a prejudiced white ear often hearing? "We want to marry your women; we want to take over your society."

Because of the phony world that many of us have been brought up in, defensive listening is a very real part of our lives. It becomes an almost automatic thing to translate what people are really saying into things that we want to hear. A good listener is a person who concentrates on what people are saying and can translate the things that he has heard into things that have some meaning for him.

e. *The balanced communicator believes in people.* He sees their pettiness, their phoniness, their projection; but he also recognizes their goodness. He tries to understand them. He doesn't classify people into good guys and bad guys, but he recognizes that everyone has something to say that is both important and worth listening to.

f. *Finally, the balanced communicator is concerned about other people.* Like everyone else, he wants people to like him, but this is not the important thing in his life. He faces people with love, but this is not the romantic, self-centered feeling type of love that we often refer to when we use this term too loosely. He is willing to hurt people when he believes that it is necessary to help them, even though he knows that they might stop liking him in the process. He is willing to talk honestly to his teachers, parents, friends, and the people whom he is concerned about. When there is something that irritates him about a person, he tells that person rather than griping about it behind his back. When he tells him, he explains that it is the irritating thing he doesn't like; not the person.

How do we become a balanced communicator? Some people have a head start in the direction of good communications by living in a home in which communications were honest and open. They have had good communications most of their lives and have been encouraged to talk about their real feelings. In other words, the feeling part of the balanced communicator has learned that healthy communications are "good" and they come easily to him.

But very few of us have this kind of experience in our growing up years. None of us have always had good experiences, simply because people are people and everyone has a great many "hang-ups" in the communication area. Becoming a balanced communicator is a constant evaluation process in which we slowly try to furnish ourselves with good communicating experiences through openness, honesty, self-evaluation, good listening, and belief and concern for other people.

Again, because people are people, even if we could reach this ideal of balanced communication, we still would have some problems in our relationships with others. Many people are afraid of the person who is open and honest; they simply don't want that much honesty.

But the benefits of good communication far outweigh the few problems that we encounter. The balanced communicator is a man who can live with himself and live with his God. Some people may not like him, but most people soon learn to trust and respect him.

Since communication is so vital to all of us, nearly everyone who reads this chapter will probably tend to ask himself the question, "Am I the strong, silent type? Am I the compulsive talker? Am I the balanced communicator?" Probably the answer that best suits most of us is that we are a blend of all three, but that we lean heavily toward one or the other. All of us have certain areas that we feel strongly about, some that we feel confident in, and some in which we feel completely lost.

In a very real sense, all of us have our pulpits. Even the silent person, for example, is silent only as long as he feels insecure in what he has to say or has a feeling that what he says will be criticized. When he discovers the area that he feels secure in, talking becomes important and much less of a problem. Compulsive talkers have had such bad experiences in some

areas that there are some things that they won't talk
about at all. They will talk at great length about something else to avoid the area that they feel is dangerous.
Yet, all of us communicate honestly in some areas. We
all have taken some stock of ourselves and have the
confidence to talk openly and honestly about some
things.

Obviously we need to achieve some sort of reasonable balance in communications and *then* get married.
The reason for this should be apparent. As we said
before, marriage is just simply living, but on a far more
concentrated basis than any other kind of life. Love
goes deeper, hurts go deeper, problems become greater
simply because we are living with them 24 hours a day.

The intense life of the married couple brings all sorts
of communication problems to the front which they
may not even have been aware of before they were
married. Nagging is far more prevalent in marriage
than most married people like to admit. It greatly
amuses me to sit with a bunch of men at a poker game
and listen to them talk about nagging as if it were a
woman's prerogative. Actually, far more young men
engage in nagging than do the women they have
married.

This is an insult to the males of this class, and I hope
that you will challenge it honestly in the observations
of the young married couples that you know. No man
ever admits that he is a nag; this is too effeminate—and
threatening to the male ego. Instead, he "helps" his
wife with "suggestions for her own good." We see him
[in his great need to help his wife] telling her how

Mother used to make the gravy or prepare the soup. He suggests many little things that she could do around the house that would improve her household standards and even offers, in his concern for her, to help her organize the household more effectively. Some men even try to tell their wives how to dress.

Sarcasm is an extremely destructive method of communicating, and again it is one that is prevalent in marriage. Nearly every home has at least one individual whose most effective defensive weapon is sarcasm.

Simply because we do not like to talk honestly *about* ourselves *to* ourselves, sarcasm is a very difficult thing to detect. It always amuses me in marriage counseling to see the reaction of a sarcastic person when you tell him that he is sarcastic. Almost universally, he responds with shock: "Who me? I'm not sarcastic. I just have a good sense of humor." The reason that we are afraid of sarcasm in ourselves, of course, is that sarcastic people are angry people and we don't like to admit hostility in ourselves. As part of the communications search that we all have to engage in all our lives, we need to constantly ask ourselves the question: "Am I a sarcastic person?" If we cannot honestly find the answer to this question, we have to go one step further and ask ourselves another: "How would I like to have these things said to me in exactly the same way?"

Neither nagging or sarcasm nor any other of the so-called "bad" traits of the human individual are necessarily wrong. Sarcasm that is used consciously can be a good thing and sometimes even a necessity, perhaps to deflate an over-inflated windbag. Nagging is something that we all need at times. There are those days when we simply wouldn't get out of bed in the morning without a little gentle nagging from someone whom we know really cares for us.

Mind reading seems to be the favorite pastime of every couple that has trouble communicating in marriage—and this includes every single couple who has ever been married. We all have some problems in this area. It is an interesting thing to sit in a counseling office and listen to two people truthfully describe the same happening. Many times it doesn't even sound like the same incident because the husband is interpreting the wife's feeling at the same time that she is interpreting his. Whenever communications break down, we engage in this mind-reading technique—and, of course, we read other people's minds from our knowledge of ourselves.

All of these things—nagging, sarcasm, mind reading —lead to a feeling of suspicion. All of us are a little insecure; it is very difficult for us to believe that people who are close to us really love us.

Whether we are married or simply looking forward to marriage, love is certainly the most important element of communications. It is a single element that above all makes our communications with people effective or ineffective. In order to talk to people in a helping kind of way, we have to really care about them. On the other hand, in order to be helped, they must know we care about them.

This is why it is so necessary that we straighten out our thinking about people (all classes and kinds of people) before we even think about maturity or marriage. We have to really like them and respect them if our conversations are to have any meaning. This is why teachers who don't care about children never succeed in teaching them; why men who don't really like women never succeed in loving women; why counselors with all kinds of degrees sometimes never succeed in counseling.

People are built through honest communications. We cannot help anyone, even ourselves, unless we are willing to open ourselves up and explain who we are and listen to who they are. We communicate only with people who *are* people, never with people who pretend to be people.

It is only when we build other people through the caring kind of communications that we reach some kind of peace with ourselves.

I think that all of us realize by now that when we talk about communications, we are discussing something that goes far deeper than just idle conversation. Those of you who have been subjected to hours and hours of religious instruction may even have become a little suspicious that we are talking about something quite religious; that this guy is really on his pulpit this time and that very soon, he is going to be talking about God again. If you had this kind of suspicion, you were correct; because, to me, communications is love, and the caring kind of communications is what Christ was talking about. None of this chapter is original. Most of it is stated in the New Testament, and I pass it on to you because I believe that Christ has suggested the only workable method of people loving people.

In our great fear of open and honest communications, we have even created a phony Christ to use as our ideal. You have all been exposed to him in the past; the Christ that was always meek, mild, and submissive, and always said nice things to nice people. We conveniently forget about the Christ who loved the Pharisees enough to tell them honestly and to their face that they were a "brood of vipers" and "whitened sepulchers" even though he knew it would hurt them.

What does all of this have to do with communications today? It has a lot to do with it. We waste far too much time feeling guilty about our honest feelings. God did not create us as sterile and passive people; He created us as real people, just as He is real people. We spend far too much time trying to stamp out what we see as "sins" in our personality: anger, hostility, frustrations. We refuse to recognize that God created all of us and what God created is good. We cannot stamp out what we are. Christian living simply means discovering what we are and then using what we discovered to love people.

The end of the "sermon" that I hope you will think about, as you are looking over your communications with everyone, deals with your communications with God as you know and understand him. I hope that these will be just as honest as your communications with other people; that you will talk to Him openly and completely. I hope that in your conversations with Him you will not be arrogant, overbearing, nagging, or boring. I hope that you will talk to Him in your own language about how you really feel about things. Whatever your concept of God may be, He is a person. Communication only takes place between people who are open and honest with each other.

DISCUSS

Classroom Discussion. This discussion is an excellent place to get rid of many of your "hang-ups" on communication, or at least to start to get rid of them. We would strongly suggest that you make this discussion a "communications laboratory." If you have been sitting silently up to this point, it might be a very good time to get involved.

Start with honesty. If you have a couple of compulsive talkers in the classroom who tend to dominate all of the conversation, or some who don't talk at all, you can be a very great help to them by telling them this. Most of us do not even realize that we talk too much or talk too little. We have built up all kinds of rationalizations about why we behave as we do so that we can keep on behaving that way. But talking too much and talking too little hurts us. This is the time to start making some changes.

The only way that you can become a better communicator yourself is to help other people with their communication problems. It's going to be a temptation for some of you who are quite sarcastic to cut the silent type down when he first starts to open up. It's all too easy for us to say, "Why don't you spit it out?" Some of the people in your classroom may have actually had such bad communication experiences that they stutter. Give them time to express themselves and listen when they do. Encourage them to keep on talking.

As you're discussing communications in the classroom, learn to listen to yourself and discover your weak points and your strong points. Be honest. This is too important an area to gloss over lightly. Talk about your own problems with communications and listen to other people's problems. One of the magic things that happens in a discussion of this type is that we discover that we all have very similar problems; that we all get deeply hurt when we don't do a good job of communicating. If you use this "communications laboratory" well, I think that you will find that it is very reassuring to you and that you're not so abnormal after all.

For your beginning discussion guide, you may simply want to refer to the things that were mentioned in the *Observe* portion of this chapter. Before you are finished, however, I hope that you will be talking about how you feel—right now—about your communications with each other in the classroom.

Discussion at Home. By now, some of you may have succeeded in establishing much better communications with your parents, while others have begun to feel hopeless. If you are having difficulty in talking with your parents, the first place that you should look for the source of the problem is at yourself. During your *Observe*, your reading of the chapter, and your self-examination in the classroom, you have been looking over your total communications with other people. You are going to want to ask yourself the same questions about talking to your parents as you asked yourself in the classroom. Some young people are sarcastic, hostile, and run away from communications in the home. It does very little good if you say, "You just can't talk to these people." You can, if you keep working at it.

Chapter VII

The Dating Process

OBSERVE

IN YOUR OBSERVATIONS FOR THIS CHAPTER, WE HOPE THAT you will pay particular attention to the younger couples that you are trying to get to know. I hope that you knew one or two of these couples before they got married. Here are some things that you can think about as you are observing them:

1. Were they in love when they got married? Was it the feeling kind of love or real love based on considerable maturity?

2. Why do you think they got married? Was it because of a deep love or was it because they wanted to get away from home? Was the girl pregnant? Was there pressure on either of them to get married?

3. Did they go together a long time before marriage? A short time? How does this seem to have affected their marriage?

Your observation of older couples can tell you something, too, about the dating process:

115

1. Are they still in love? Does the man still court his wife? Does he take her out quite often and seem very proud of her?

2. Should dating continue in marriage? Do you think that it does in most homes you have observed?

OBSERVE II

The behavior of young people reflects the way that they get along at home. Perhaps you would like to take a look at your three friends and their dating behavior. If there are other people whom you know quite well, you might want to compare their dating behavior to that of your friends:

1. Do the people whom you are observing get along well at home?

2. Do you think that their treatment of the boys or girls they are with reflects their feeling toward their parents, sisters, or brothers?

3. If they are rebellious toward their parents, how does it show up in their dating behavior?

Since dating is a very important part of the lives of many juniors and seniors, you will probably want to go much deeper in your observations on this chapter and take a look at the dating patterns of the people whom you see around you in both the school and the neighborhood. Here are some things that I hope you will observe:

1. Are many of your classmates going steady?

2. If quite a few are, are most of them preparing for marriage? Are their preparations realistic?

3. Are there many pressures among young adults your age toward going steady? Do your friends treat you any differently when they discover that you are steady dating?

4. Are quite a few of the young couples having sexual intercourse? Are these the mature couples or the less mature in your acquaintances?

The final part of your *Observe* should be yourself and how you feel about all of the above questions. Since this program is an experiment in honesty, we hope that you will give considerable thought to your dating practices and feelings as you are making your observations of other people and carefully thinking through the material in the chapter.

Discovering real love isn't easy

An unwilling husband once described the dating process as "that exciting and deadly game." This may sound a little negative, but it certainly has some truth. The dating years are definitely exciting years. But, on the other hand, there are serious moments, too, in which you will find out about yourself and how you fit with other people. Obviously, some place during the dating process you will find that one person who complements you so well that you will want to spend the rest of your life with him (or her).

Only one reason for getting married makes sense to me, and this is the only one we will talk about. The only reason any two people should marry is that they are in love. Love, however, is a confusing term. Through our music, our movies, our novels, our television and commercials, it is frequently associated with "feeling good." The concept of "instant love" is very thoroughly rooted in America; the hope that someday, somehow, we will find this individual who really sends us.

Feeling good about each other is, of course, an essential ingredient of married love. Yet it is a small part of what love means. We can talk about dating much more honestly if we first face the fact that boys feel good to girls and girls feel good to boys and that both of these varieties of people feel extremely good to each other when they are in each other's arms.

The love that we need to make a marriage work has a great many more dimensions than just the feeling part. We need to have the feeling that we want to give ourselves to the other party and to serve him. We need respect for ourselves and each other. We need the joy of just simply being with each other even when there is no contact at all. We need to be able to communicate on every level and about everything. All of these things are the purpose of dating; to find this individual that we complement and who complements us so that we not only want to be with each other, but we *need* to be with each other.

As a marriage counselor, it always amazes me to see the number of people who blunder into matrimony with just the feeling part of love. Not so long ago, we had a couple come into the office for counseling who were married just three weeks. They had already discovered that they did not even know each other. Neither of them, of course, had any idea of what maturity or responsibility meant or even that these were important in a marriage relationship.

If the only valid reason for marrying a person is that you love him, we can begin to understand why so many marriages break down. Sometimes the people whom we see in counseling really loved each other when they said, "I do." But many times their marriage was based on all kinds of reasons that have nothing whatsoever to do with love and that certainly have nothing whatsoever to do with maturity.

We can't actually blame anyone for these kinds of marriages. The people who made them sincerely felt that they were doing what was best for them. Some young people have been literally forced into marriage because they knew nothing about themselves and nothing about each other as sexual persons.

We see this lack of knowledge constantly in the kind of written questions that are turned in in our sex education program. In our office we have several hundred questions in feminine handwriting which say: "How do you turn a guy off?" and "Why do boys get 'turned on' so quickly?" The answer to these is simple: The thing that turns boys on is girls. Girls naturally want and need signs of affection; they like to be held and loved. Boys who can't understand this in women sometimes completely misinterpret the girl's actions and feel that any display of affection on her part is an invitation to sexual intercourse. Too many people get married to "solve" this problem. Marriage doesn't solve it, of course. Their lack of knowledge of the sexuality of each other is what caused it in the first place.

The sexual trap is usually only a small part of the reason why many people marry without real love. A great many young people are either unconsciously or consciously attempting to escape from problems at home. Some of these problems are natural ones and occur in any family. Girls grow up to be young ladies. Suddenly, instead of mother and daughter, we have two women in the home. This never works very well. The same thing is true of boys who grow up to be young men and find that they have ideas of their own that are very much in conflict with their father's. Communications often break down at this time, and marriage looks like a good alternative to the tension that they feel around them.

Some young people feel unwanted at home. In a few rare instances, they probably are unwanted. But in most cases this is, again, simply a problem of communications; two parents who do not know how to express their feelings to their children. Many girls, in particular, get married out of an exaggerated need for love that comes straight out of their childhood. Perhaps there has been no affection in the home even between the parents, or perhaps, again, the parents simply haven't known how to express it. At any rate, a lot of girls dream of marriage as a place in which they can receive all of the love that they have missed for most of their life.

Some people move into marriage more quickly than they want to simply because of the social pressures exerted on them by their young friends around them. "Everybody's doing it," can have a lot more effect on the way we feel than we like to admit.

Fortunately, the romance trap of your parents' generation is rather quickly disappearing. Young people today are becoming much more aware of the fact that a lifetime together is not necessarily a lifetime of holding hands in the moonlight. The love songs of the younger generation tend to be more realistic; yet even today a lot of fantasy about marriage exists. The basic falseness of these fantasies is the idea that "love comes to us." Mature love is not a receiving kind of thing. Mature love is something we build.

But all of the above are a fairly normal part of most decisions to marry. It's good to have dreams. As long as they are not exaggerated too badly, none of them are really dangerous. The marriages that get in serious trouble are the ones that are created to solve major problems in the personality of the individual. These are the despair of every marriage counselor.

Very frequently, for example, we see the young man or the young woman who has a real hang-up with Dad or Mom and is extremely rebellious and hostile. Their whole dating pattern is a rebellion against the standards that their parents claim to stand for. They move into sexual intercourse quickly and "have themselves a ball" simply because of the fact that what they are doing would give their parents fits. They find ecstasy here—and they get married suddenly. What has been so much fun before becomes legal and has to be based on a mature relationship, and they find themselves living with nothing but hatred and rebellion upon which to build their future.

There are many other marriages that are made simply to work out childhood feelings. The son or daughter of an alcoholic parent, for example, will want to give long and serious consideration to his or her reasons for wanting to marry. It is not accidental that many girls with alcoholic parents tend to marry heavy drinkers. They have always wanted to help Daddy with his problem and have felt very guilty because they have not succeeded. Unconsciously, they sometimes try to work out their feelings about Daddy by sacrificing their lives to another drinking problem.

One of our cynical psychiatrists who had been faced with a constant parade of marriage break-ups once made this statement: "The only two people who can live together are a sadist and a masochist." Briefly stated, a sadist is a person who wants to punish someone and a masochist a person who feels so guilty that he wants to be punished. Unfortunately, we see these neurotic patterns in marriage a lot more often than any of us care to admit or even think about. We see the man who brutally beats his wife, for example, who, in turn, meekly submits and displays her suffering for all of the world to see. She actually gets some sick pleasure out of her beating.

None of these people are in love. It is simply not possible for them to *be* in love. No one can ever love another person unless he first has love for himself. He has nothing to give until then.

None of the above problems should discourage the person about eventually marrying. They simply mean that he or she is a long way from maturity and that these problems have to be worked out before marriage can even be considered. This is exactly what dating is all about; getting to know ourselves with both our strengths and weaknesses and preparing ourselves for a marriage that is real. It means growing up, and in the process, locating another grown-up to live with and love for the rest of our lives. What does this process involve?

First of all, it involves many experiences with many people. This is just good common sense—everything about marriage is common sense. Marriage is a constant association with people, and it only makes sense to thoroughly explore what kind of people we will find ourselves comfortable with. Marriage is forty or fifty or sixty years of looking at the same person across the breakfast table.

Most often, the dating process involves many loves for many people. This is real, too. There is no greater myth than the one that says that one man loves one

woman only and that one woman loves one man only
for all of their lives. During the forty or fifty years that
they live together, a man who has no particular hang-
ups on women will feel many different kinds of loves
for many different women and the woman will feel
many different kinds of loves for many men. These loves,
of course, are different and far less complete than the
fulfilling love that a man has for the one special woman
that he chooses to marry. Nevertheless, they are real;
the only way to distinguish between these kinds of love
and the one that grows stronger all through life is to
actually experience them. Many loves, of course, generally mean many hurts. This, too, is good and part of
the normal process of becoming a mature individual.

The dating process also involves "going steady"—perhaps many times—before a man and a woman finally
decide that this is for keeps and for life; there is no one
else that they want to live with.

I suppose that many of you have been warned often
by both parents and teachers of the dangers of "going
steady." You probably feel that this author is some sort
of traitor to the "Stone Age generation" to even suggest
that this is a necessary part of the dating process. However, both young adults and their parents have wasted
far too much emotion on "going steady." As a matter of
fact, I sometimes think that many of the problems that
have come about are a direct response to the almost
hysterical insistence of the parents that, "None of our
kids are going to go steady." There is a quite natural
teenage rebellion against this authority. One of the
things that I hope both parents and teenagers will do

as a part of this program is to take a look at their feelings in this touchy area and talk about them.

The idea that men and women can somehow get to know each other and discover who they are through simply "traveling with the crowd" or dating a different person every night is totally unrealistic.

What does going steady really mean? What people should say when they decide to spend a lot of time together is this: "I think that this is the kind of person I could really like, and I want to find out for sure." If it is accompanied by a realistic appraisal of the two individuals' maturity and readiness for marriage, it can and should be a healthy thing. Perhaps it is a great deal more than that, though. It may be the *only* way that two people can discover the kind of person that they really like.

Unfortunately, most parents go into a complete panic about the fourth or fifth time that their son (or daughter) goes out with the same young man (or young lady). Their reasons for this panic are simple and are universal. Jeanette and I go into the same kind of panic when our own teenagers start the steady dating pattern. Our problem is that we never really have enough confidence in ourselves and in the job that we have done in raising them. Young people feel that we do not trust them, and perhaps this is true. But the people that we really mistrust are ourselves. By this time of life, all parents are acutely aware of the many times that they have failed in their communications with their children. We know that we have protected them too much or ignored them too much or that we have not given them as much love as we would have liked to, or that we have not provided a very good example. These are the real reasons for the parental panic over "steady dating." We want you to have better experiences than we had in the early years of our marriage and we are tremendously afraid that we have not given you the confidence and knowledge that you will need to cope with your sexuality and to wait for maturity before going to the altar or to bed.

I think that we all have to face the fact that communications between generations is generally not very good. This causes all kinds of misunderstandings. I am quite sure that the average teenager believes that he reads us very clearly when he sees our fears showing through on steady dating. What he reads is in bold, bright print: "You don't trust us." I am quite sure, too, that at least a few young people continue with a worn-out steady simply because of the fact that they are reacting to their parents.

But the trap part of steady dating is not just rebellion against parents. There are also a lot of pressures from teens themselves. When a girl is "tagged" as a steady, most boys leave her strictly alone. She isn't even asked for a date. Sometimes she hangs onto the boy that she has because she feels that there is no one else in sight. The young couple who has been going steady for a while is also aware of the fact that they are going to go through considerable criticism from their friends if and when they do decide to break up. Sometimes, too, it can be reassuring to know that you always have a date available for a dance or a party. It is easier to simply keep the whole thing going, even after it has lost its interest, than it is to stop and start over.

The thing that everyone fears (and almost no one talks about) is the thought of premarital sexual intercourse and the kind of thing that often happens in this kind of relationship. Sexual intercourse is a tremendous emotional experience and, as we have mentioned many times before, needs always to be approached with a great deal of maturity and love if it is to have a good effect on the personality.

If the young couple is really mature and really in love, sexual intercourse is not as great a problem. They have a great deal of respect for themselves and each other, knowledge of what marriage is all about, and a very strong desire to make the first act of sexual intercourse a loving kind of sex.

I think that teenagers have to face some facts, too. One of these is that there is not much mature love involved in much of the steady dating. Many young people have no real concept of themselves and the people they are with. Some do not even understand the basic sexuality or the feelings involved. In far too many cases, the decision to go steady is based on the fact that the boy or the girl they select is "cool," or "tough." Once the dating pattern begins, they find that they actually have little in common and not much to talk about.

Young adults, like old adults, are constantly searching for love, but few adults of any age have ever discovered what it means. It is much easier, for example, to explore the feeling part of love than it is to take a look at ourselves and at each other through communication. Some "steadies" start their dates with necking and petting, probably because it is the "in" thing to do. Maybe they neck and pet because they don't really know how to talk with each other; they just want to have a good time and find love.

The feeling part of love comes very easily, but quickly it becomes a trap in which sexual contact becomes the reason for continuing to steady date and the thing that young couples are thinking about constantly. Obviously, there is no maturity and no real love involved in a relationship that simply "feels good."

If maturity is the thing that young couples are looking for, steady dating is good, but has to involve real communications on every level. They have to discover: "Is this the kind of person that I really like?" and the only way to do this is to find out what kind of person they are going with.

A lot of "hog-wash" about dating and courtship has been published by adults who should have known better. They were honestly afraid of the sexual intercourse trap that can stop the growth of a real relationship between a boy and a girl. When we grew up, a lot of people talked about the "chaste kiss" as the absolute limit that young people could explore before marriage. The chaste kiss was a sort of sanitized and desexualized peck on the lips that didn't involve the emotions at all. This was so totally unrealistic that our generation, like yours, completely rejected it. I have never seen a successful marriage that was based on a "chaste kiss" relationship. It is just as necessary to discover how you feel about each other as it is to discover what you are in every other way.

If the young couple ever hopes to grow up, however, the feeling part of love has to develop as mature love deepens. Young people need to talk about everything. Just how much talking takes place in the back seat of a car when the boy's hand is on the girl's breast?

It is not possible to love a person whom you do not respect. Respect leads to better control simply because you do not want to hurt your marriage.

I sincerely like the young people who are growing up today. They are well educated, more thoughtful, and more concerned with people than any generation before them has ever been. Yet, I also have a great deal of sympathy for them. It must be an extremely confusing time in which to mature. Nothing is as clear-cut as it seemed to be 20 or 25 years ago.

The whole area of contact between the sexes must be confusing. On the one hand, you are faced with the fear merchants who are constantly warning you about venereal diseases and illegitimate pregnancies. On the other hand, you are faced with hundreds of books written by so-called "authorities" on sex who paint a vivid picture of how happy you can be if you just practice all of the good techniques.

Yet, I have a great deal of confidence in young people, too. This confidence was hard to come by because I belong to the hung-up generation. Nearly all young people today are at least wanting to put sex in its only logical place—a loving, permanent relationship. The hurting kind of sex which involves conquering women is quickly being abandoned. If we adults can bring ourselves to level with you people, I believe that you are fully capable of making responsible decisions. You are not fools; you are well aware of the disasters that result from the "hippie" experimentations with "free sex." I cannot believe that you will be confused by eminent authorities whose personal lives are a mess. You want more from sex than just excitement.

Discovering real love can be a hard, tough business. Yet, as we have said before, it is the only possible way of living with yourself. It brings a reward of deep contentment.

There are many visions of what the world that you young people will create will be like. Many of them claim to be religious. One of them is the vision of the Jansenists and the Puritans, which says that man was conceived in original sin. He is basically evil and there will always be trouble, hatred, and wars.

The other great vision is the vision of Christ, of a world united in love.

I believe that both of these visions are true, but both of them start with people. They continue in homes in which children are taught to love or are taught to hate. If you young people can get rid of your "hang-ups" of dishonesty and really learn to communicate, understand, and accept each other, it is entirely possible to create a world in which people know how to love one another.

DISCUSS

Classroom Discussion. Once again, we would like to suggest that you use the questions listed in the *Observe* portion as a take-off point for your discussion in the classroom. However, we hope that by now you will trust each other enough to begin to go much deeper than that. Perhaps now you will be ready to discuss your own feelings about dating, about steady dating, about marriage, and about premarital sexual intercourse. Keep in mind that this is your group and that you owe considerable loyalty to the members of it. Young adults are always complaining about phoniness and fakery of the adult world. There doesn't have to be any phoniness or fakery here. If the discussions have been going well, you already feel very close to several members of your class. This always happens when people care enough to talk honestly with each other. There may be some members in the class who want to share their problems with you. This experience is human and it can be very beautiful.

Discussion at Home. Many crises arise between young people and parents over dating practices. If there have been some problems in your home, this is as good a time as any to start to come to grips with them. Many parents feel very hopeless in coping with young people during this time. Many young people rebel against what they believe are unrealistic limits set by their parents. They regard their parents as old fashioned and out of tune with the times. This may well be—if you haven't helped them keep up with the times by telling it like it is in the home.

If you are willing to tell your parents what you do and where you go and whom you are with, most parents are much more willing to talk about time to be in, use of the car, and so on. Decisions regarding your dating practices should be shared responsibilities by the time that you are juniors and seniors, but no parent can do a very good job of sharing this responsibility with you if he has no idea of what your dating life is like. Some give up on it and seem to let you do as you please; some attempt to be overly strict. All of these things are as much your problem as they are the problem of your parents.

Many students try to come up with some dating standards in discussions of this type. If your class seems to be working around toward these, this is again an excellent time to tell your parents what you are doing. Keep in mind what we have said about communications all the way through this book. When any two people who love each other are not talking to each other as they should, there is always distrust. If your parents distrust you, it probably is a communication problem and one that you can do something about.

Chapter VIII

The Honeymoon:
What It Is
and What It Can Be

OBSERVE

SOME OF YOU MAY BE VERY WELL ACQUAINTED BY NOW
with the people whom you have been observing. If you
are, and if you feel comfortable with them, you might
want to see if you can get them reminiscing about their
own honeymoon. Encourage them by listening carefully. It is always better to have the wife and husband
together at a time like this, because you can then detect
how they react toward each other during the telling.

Most of you may not feel that comfortable with your
couples. If not, you are going to have to rely to a certain extent on the younger couples whom you know
personally. Some of these may be brothers or sisters or
close relatives.

Regardless of how you approach it, there is one thing
that you will particularly want to notice in observing
their relationship to each other and in trying to get
some idea of what living together is like. This is the
area of compatibility. Some counselors suggest that all
of us should look for a mate who likes the same kinds

of things that we do. They even go so far in some cases as to try to match personalities with computers. One of the best ways to find out just how compatible people are is to observe them. Here are some "compatibility tests" that you can administer to each of the couples whom you are observing:

1. Do both enjoy the same outdoor activities?

2. Do both of them enjoy dancing? Do they like the same kinds of dances?

3. Are both of them quite outgoing? Or, is one of them quite introverted?

4. Are both equally capable of handling money?

5. Do both seem to have their "high" periods at the same time of the day and both have their "low" periods at the same time?

6. Do they both have the same ideas about dress and style?

7. Are their ideas on disciplining children approximately the same?

8. Do they agree on decorating plans for their household?

9. Are their political leanings the same?

10. Are they both equally neat in dress and appearance?

11. Do they both like to read? Both like to watch TV?

You will probably be able to think up at least as many compatibility tests of your own. It is very important that you observe carefully and decide whether compatibility in marriage is possible.

OBSERVE II

Take a look at those friends of yours and see what members of the opposite sex they are attracted to. Many times we like to think about "the perfect match": boys and girls who seem to share nearly all of the same things. But, is this what happens when your friends start dating?

A period
of adjustment

Honeymoon is a very deceiving term and one which
is not very easy to define. According to the American
myth of marriage, it is a period of intense happiness.
It is sort of a dream-world stage that is supposed to
continue through all our lives. This actually happens
in a very few marriages; perhaps one in 10,000 marriages. But for most of us, the honeymoon is a period
of adjustment. It can be very difficult at times and very
joyful at times. It is that time in which we stop dream-
ing about living together and start living together 24
hours a day. Your own experiences have already taught
you that life is quite different from the dreams that you
have about life simply because life is real and people
are real.

Most people start marriage with wonderful possibilities. They have a powerful young love with a lot of
exuberance and trust and believe in themselves and
their love. Yet, even the strength of this love and the
deep feeling for each other presents a few possibilities
of pain.

The key ingredient that needs to be added to young
marriage to make it grow and develop into something
as beautiful as all of us want it to be is, again, maturity.
Maturity always means facing life honestly as it is and
moving into a real world of love that you created,

rather than a dream world of love that is somehow going to just come.

Thirty years ago it was not possible for young people to move easily into a real world of marriage. We had no idea at all what to expect—for most of us, the only premarital counseling that we received was five minutes with a priest or minister. He told us to have faith in God, to pray hard, and to pray together as a family. We wandered into marriage completely blind and then struggled for ten or more years before we even began to understand the person that we had married. Like all young people everywhere, we spent hours and hours looking at the moon and telling each other that ours would be different, without even the vaguest notion of what it was that we were going to make different. This was not just our generation. People have blundered into marriage for thousands of years. Perhaps the greatest myth of all times was the one that said that people need to be prepared to be a mechanic, school teacher, or welder—but marriage is something that just works out because we love each other.

This myth was so strong that it even penetrated our churches, and it is still very much alive in them today. If we were to ask any priest or minister the following two questions, we could expect the same response from all of them. This is what Christians believe. The first question is this:

"What is the basic message of Christ?" Each priest and minister would answer, "That we love God and love one another."

If we followed up with the second question, "Where is the best place to build this love?", the answer again would be unanimous, "In the home."

Yet, even though nearly all priests and ministers would quickly agree that love is built in the home, the strength of the myth is that people can find out how to do this all by themselves. This is evidenced by the fact that even today less than 50 percent of the churches in America have an organized system of marriage education and marriage preparation. As few as ten years ago, this figure would have been less than 10 percent.

Meanwhile, all of the sicknesses of marriage are becoming more and more apparent. Huge numbers experience symptoms of marital illness: divorces, family disorganization, unwed pregnancies, homosexuality, juvenile delinquency, and crime.

I have seen the many hang-ups on sexual maturity that the people of the older generation have had, and I have tried to communicate them to you in this program. Yet, in a very real sense, I am proud of our generation because, for the first time in history, we are looking past the myth and starting to realize the potentials of marriage. We have always said that the home is a basic unit of any society and that the strength of the society depends upon the strength of the home. But, up until now, no one has done anything about strengthening the home or has even considered the possibilities that it has for creating love. Today, if he wants to, nearly every person has an opportunity to receive some kind of premarital education. A lot of it is not very good as yet, but at least it is a great deal more than we ever have had before. You have the opportunity of going into marriage with your eyes wide open, but still a little dreamy. This is the kind of combination that it takes to build a really solid relationship.

A lot of things happen to you on a honeymoon that are completely different from the things that happen to anyone else simply because of the fact that you are yourselves and are different from everyone else. But it helps a great deal if you have some idea of the real things that happen to two young people in their initial adjustment to each other. With this information, you can talk now and at least have some idea of how you are going to cope with them if and when they begin to happen to you.

Part of what I like to call the "shock" of marriage stems from the phoniness of much of the dating process in America. It simply is not honest in many ways. When a boy drops in to a girl's house to pick her up, she "looks like a million bucks" and this is no accident; she spent considerable time and money getting to look that way. Her whole self concentrated on impressing this man that she loves. Since she is not with him on a 24-hour-a-day basis, it is not hard to be the kind of person that she thinks he wants her to be.

Who is more dishonest than a young man who is courting a woman that he is in love with? Again, he tells her all kinds of things that he knows that she wants to hear, and he paints her a picture of a lifetime of loving attention.

It is natural and normal to want to impress each other. We do love each other a great deal. But it is very disillusioning when we move out of this stage and into real marriage. There we discover that many things we believed to be real about our lover were really a "show" that was put on for our benefit. The shock of reality is especially damaging if the engagement period is short with a lot of sexual involvement and no real communications.

Jeanette and I have finally reached the stage in which we can look back together at the things that we both discovered on our honeymoon and laugh about them without any hurt. But they were not so funny at the time. Even today we have a little trouble discussing some of the really terrible things that happened to us sexually—because of my complete lack of knowledge of her as a woman and her lack of knowledge of me as a man. In some of these instances, the hurt and misunderstanding went very deep and took a long time to work out.

The little things we can really laugh about. For example, in her family, steak was cooked to a crisp; in ours it was served with the blood still running. She is a person who wakes up jolly and happy; I am a person who does not like anyone (not even myself) the first thing in the morning.

All of these little realities that happen to people make it hard to talk to each other because we are afraid. Sometimes we are not even too sure who we are talking to. A hundred small irritations crop up that are completely unexpected and further hurt our communications. It is very disillusioning for a woman to discover, for example, that her husband snores or perhaps burps at the dinner table. It is disillusioning, also, to discover that this great lover of hers who always wanted to sit and hold her all night before they were married comes home from the office tired and crabby, tunes in the television, and just wants to be left alone.

It is sometimes hard for a husband to understand how his wife could really like her mother. It is hard, too, for him to understand how those wonderful meals that she cooked for him (with the help of her mother), suddenly degenerate into TV dinners.

But all of these are little things. With them are some real basic personality differences that occur in every marriage. It takes a lot of understanding and love to handle these differences.

We have talked a great deal about men and women complementing each other, and this complementary relationship is the only solid basis for marriage. We hear a great deal about compatibility; these people have the same likes and dislikes. Very often, before marriage, they do: They both like to hold each other. But two people who are really compatible simply could not make a marriage work. In a real sense, all of us have unbalanced personalities, and we tend to choose our mates because they have strengths where we have weaknesses, and we have strengths where they have weaknesses. In other words, we marry people because we need them and they need us.

We need a person who is very different than we are, and we deliberately select one who is. Yet, it is still very hard to accept someone who thinks differently than we do, has different ideas of the importance of things, and even acts in a way that we are completely unfamiliar with. From our own experiences, we decide that a certain way of behaving is the right way to behave; and this person we married does not behave in that way. This is a real threat to us because if we agree that maybe her way could be the right way, we have to take a hard look at our own selves and make some basic changes. At this point, we become afraid that this suddenly strange person we are married to will walk over us and make us change. It seems much more logical to change the person we are married to rather than ourselves.

This is why every new marriage goes through a long testing period. It is a good and normal thing in which both people should be trying to discover exactly who they are married to and what kind of pattern they will be setting for this new marriage. However, it becomes a good and healthy thing only if these young people are able to approach each other with maturity, understanding, and patience. If they do not, then each of these new differences can become a crisis.

The first payday, for example, is a critical time in every new home. Somebody wants to pay all of the bills and somebody wants to make a down-payment on a new car. Neither party wants to give in very easily. Sunday afternoon can be another kind of crisis in which the husband wants to watch the football game, and the wife wants to go for a drive. The first evening out can become a crisis—when they were single, the husband liked his wife to be dressed nice and sexy; but now he's not so sure about that. The first time they decide to talk things over sometimes does not work very well because one of them pouts and will not talk at all, which leads to the other's ranting, raving, and shouting. Very few men know how to cope with a woman in tears—it is very frustrating to them. Yet, every man is faced with a woman in tears many times during the first few months of marriage.

Many of these tears appear because of the real frustrations that occur in every young marriage in the sexual area. As we will see from later chapters, the sexual myth is probably the greatest myth of all. The basis of the myth is that everything else between the couple can be wrong, yet they have this thing to pull them back together again.

Most women go into marriage believing that every act of sexual intercourse is an act of love. This is what it should be, of course. Yet, unless the young man and the young woman really mature and really communicate in this and every other level before they are married, their sexual relationship has many other meanings besides love; and most of these are hurting kinds of meanings.

1. For most young men, sex is a proving ground for their ego. They have been indoctrinated all of their lives with the belief that every man can satisfy the woman that he loves. If it were simply satisfaction that they were seeking here, this would present no major problems because every relationship can and should be satisfying to her if there is love involved in it.

But when we are talking about a full climax in the woman, we are generally talking about something else again. This may occur accidentally during the first few months of marriage, or it may occur at a time when she feels especially loving. In extremely rare cases of exceptionally mature men and women who really have searched themselves and gotten rid of their hang-ups on sex, it may occur quite often. But in most homes, it does not occur at all during the first few months or even years of marriage.

The reasons for this should be quite obvious from the things that we have talked about up to this point. We do not get rid of all of our feelings about sex and about men and women simply by saying a few words and going to bed with each other. It takes a lot of love, understanding, and respect to work out a satisfying relationship. Even a climax in marriage is something that has to be built; it is not something that just happens.

In some few cases, it may occur quite frequently on the honeymoon simply because of the intensity of the feelings of the first love-making. If this happens, the couple is fortunate. But they will also need a great deal of maturity to accept the fact that it may take years and years of getting to know each other before the same kind of relationship develops again.

All of this is extremely upsetting to the man who believes that this should happen every night or that somehow his failure to bring his wife to a climax means that he is not much of a man. This rather typical male attitude is just plain silly; yet, it is the attitude that most men bring to their honeymoon.

2. If the man feels that he is sexually inadequate, he quickly develops an obsession or a hang-up on this and worries about it. We will be discussing some of the things that happen to him in more detail later. But with the newly married man, worry and concern about his sexual performance most generally results in a great need to prove himself sexually. The penis of the man is simply an instrument of his brain; and if he thinks about sex a great deal, the penis erects often. For this reason, many young married men are extremely aggressive sexually, so much so that the wives come up with a great disgust with the whole thought of sex and lay the groundwork for future frigidity.

3. If the man has very little understanding of himself and is quite insecure to begin with, the first frustrating experiences with sex lead very quickly to impotency. It takes a rather strange form in the male. He can have an erection at any time during the day, but is not able to sustain this erection when it is time to insert the penis into the vagina. If we think about this just a minute, we will quickly recognize what is happening. The mind of the man is saying to the organ of the man, "This is going to be another frustrating experience. Don't try it." Here we have the situation in which he prepares his wife for sexual intercourse and then is not able to perform. This is very frustrating to her.

4. If the initial experiences with sex are not satis-

fying, the woman, too, has some real problems with guilt. After all, she does love her man, and she wants him to be happy and contented. She, too, has usually been conditioned to believe that every man can do this. Instead of recognizing that the problem between them is simply one of lack of knowledge and understanding, her immediate reaction is, "What is the matter with me?" When this happens, she goes into the relationship with all kinds of fears and doubts which make it even harder for her to respond to him and again increases her guilty feelings.

5. Sometimes men and women both need sexual relationships simply as a release of tension. Quite often this happens when one or the other simply cannot get in the mood. If they can talk about sex honestly, this presents no problems and generally will lead to an even greater feeling of love between the two of them. If they are not communicating, however, one or the other will feel that they are being "used."

6. Sometimes sex is used as a weapon. Since feelings go so deep in this area and responses are so strong, it offers a convenient way of really hurting each other. The woman, for example, may approach her man at a time when she knows he will not be able to perform. Or he may approach her brutally with no loving preparation at all. I think that all of you will recognize that this kind of behavior is extremely childish. It really destroys the love that they both want and need. Yet we are human and sometimes we are childish. This does happen in many marriages.

I think that you will realize in the above that sexual intercourse has many faces. It can and should be the climax of all the love that you bring into your honeymoon. But it also can be the thing that destroys your love and becomes the most detested element of your marriage. It is bad or good, but it is always powerful. The direction that it takes is entirely up to you.

We spent a great deal of time in this book on sex and its implications only because of the fact that this is an area in which we have all been taught so badly. I believe that twenty-five years from now, we may not have to discuss sex at all in a book of this type. It is a simple thing that should happen naturally. It is not a thing that requires any deep-seated knowledge. Good sexual relationships are simply the method of expressing your maturity.

The reality of living with a person 24 hours a day can be a frightening thing to think about. To those of you who are thinking about marriage as an escape from something, I hope it will be frightening. When two immature people marry, the results are sheer misery. If you are honest in your observations, I am sure that you will see this in some of your friends who married on the basis of the feeling kind of love.

Yet for those of you who are willing to learn to talk with each other and come to grips with yourselves, the first few years of marriage can really be a honeymoon. Regardless of how mature you may be, there will be many hurts and a great deal of disillusion. Yet with all of this, there is also the strength of love and confidence in yourselves and each other. There is a feeling that now there are two of you to complement each other and to make you stronger than one person could ever be.

There is only one person who can judge your maturity and readiness for marriage. This one person is *you*.

DISCUSS

Classroom Discussion

1. Why do you think that compatibility was stressed so much during the *Observe* and during the chapter?

2. If you have been doing your homework and have been talking in your classroom the way that we hope you have talked, you probably know each other better by now than you know any other people. As a break in the routine, you might like to try something different that can help you understand a great deal about a honeymoon and the things that you can expect from it.

Select a boy and a girl from your class who seem to be communicating very well. It will help if these two people have some acting ability. The boy can play the role of a husband who is married for four weeks. The girl will be his wife.

From your observations, give a little thought to the parts that they will play. First of all, we have to assume that they love each other deeply. But, secondly, we have to also remember that this is a real situation and that both have brought their personalities into marriage. In the classroom situation, they have already found some things that they like about each other and some things that they don't like.

The scene that this "married couple" can play is a breakfast table on the anniversary of their first month of marriage. If you prefer to set it up in some other way, however, feel free. This is your discussion and it should be based on your experiences. After the couple has completed acting out their parts, you may want to all join in with your suggestions on what the honeymoon is like and how two people react to each other after they have lived together, as intensely as they do in marriage, for thirty days.

Discussion at Home. If you are now finding it easier to talk with your parents, you have probably discovered that they will be using considerable humor when talking about the honeymoon. Tell them that you're discussing it in school and perhaps even describe your role-playing episode humorously. It's good for your parents to talk about their honeymoon; it's good for you to hear them talk about it.

Chapter IX

The Opposite Sex?

OBSERVE

TO BEGIN TO GET SOME REAL UNDERSTANDING OF THE people whom you are observing, this one will have to be done carefully. In some cases, you are going to have to go considerably deeper than what appears to be on the surface. It is possible that this is the time in our history when young adults can discard the myths of "The Opposite Sex" and finally begin to understand that both men and women are people. The observation part of this chapter can again form the basis of your discussion. Yet, I hope that your discussion will be on a much more personal level and that girls will tell the boys who they are and the boys will respond in kind. You can get rid of some real "hang-ups" on masculinity and femininity if you observe honestly and then later discuss honestly. We can't even tell you what you might discover: You probably already know as much about the meaning of masculinity and femininity as we do:

1. Is the man whom you are observing able to express his love and concern to his wife and family? Does

his manner of expressing it lead to a hurting kind of relationship or a loving one?

2. Is the man's appearance "masculine"? Does this make any difference to the relationship?

3. Does he have contempt for women or appreciation of them? Does this hurt or help the people whom he loves? Does he seem to feel superior to his wife? Inferior to her? What does this do to the marriage?

In your *Observe* group, we hope that there is at least one relationship that all of your feelings tell you is good and sound. Carefully observe this man and try to determine what manliness means to him. Compare him with the other men in your *Observe* group and with the ideas you might have brought into this program about manliness.

Use the same kind of observation on the wives. Find the woman who says with her whole life that she is happily married. Contrast her with the women who are not so happily married and with the concepts of women that you may have received through movies, television, and even in the classroom.

Finally, you might want to compare and contrast in your own mind the mature, happily married woman and the mature, happily married man.

Balancing the roles
of man and woman

One of the most surprising things that we see in marriage counseling is the fact that men and women know so little about each other after many thousands of years of living together. Man after man comes into the office and tells me, "You cannot reason with her," and woman after woman comes into the office and says, "All he thinks about is himself." It becomes easier to understand why there is such confusion between the two when we realize that for thousands and thousands of years men and women did not talk to each other honestly. Very few men have ever really had the opportunity of getting to know a woman, and very few women have had this same opportunity with men.

The damage done to the human race by this great misunderstanding between men and women has been tremendous. For thousands of years the world has been ruled by men, and the "opposite sex" has had almost no opportunity of growing and developing and contributing to the world around her. Even in modern twentieth-century America, we still have all kinds of hangovers from the Dark Ages when women were second-class citizens. I think that most of you young men have heard expressions like these from other young men; perhaps you've heard them in your own home: "A woman's place is in the home," "If you want her happy, keep her barefoot and pregnant," or even, "They are nice for loving; but for heaven's sake, don't try to talk to them."

For thousands of years, too, the woman was considered to be a sexually neutral person whose task in life was to please man. We painted images of the self-sacrificing mother who was always there to go to bed with her man when he wanted to go to bed. Her "joy" was in raising his children, jumping whenever he asked her to jump, but still worshiping the ground that he walked on.

With this mass potential of more than one half of the human race almost completely untapped, is it any wonder that the human race has never really learned to love one another?

As marriage has been around since the dawn of civilization, I really believe that all of human history can be traced back to one man and one woman and how they felt about each other. If every man and every woman could look at each other and like what they saw, then every child would grow up in a home surrounded by love. This child would never hate his neighbor or foreigners or Catholics or Protestants or Jews, because he had been taught to love, *not* to hate.

If we think about the "good old days" we will realize that they probably were not so good after all. The reason should be obvious. The woman, too, is a human being with all of the same feelings that a man has. She likes to be loved, and she likes to be led. But she does not like to be ordered around any more than any other person.

I hope that in the *Discuss* portion of this chapter, all of you young adults will talk over thoroughly your feelings about authority. It does men, in particular, a great deal of good to discover that women are certainly no different from men in this respect. When either men or women are pushed, they tend to push back because they are people, and people need to be loved and respected.

Can there really be any respect for the human being in a home in which the mother is a nothing? Is it really possible for a woman to love a man she cannot even argue with or discuss things with? Is it possible for *you* to love a person who does not respect you? Would the average woman in this kind of home teach love to her children through the way she acted toward her husband, or would she perhaps teach hatred?

What kind of children come out of this authoritarian type of home? Certainly not many well-balanced ones. As you know from your own experiences, children who are raised in a home in which there is completely unreasonable authority tend to become either very hostile and angry people or very submissive people. If someone makes all of their decisions for them, the children discover as they grow older that they are not capable of making decisions for themselves. They have to have a dictator—someone who will tell them what to do. They feel more comfortable with a dictator who suppresses and degrades other people because this is what Daddy did in his home all his life.

It is even possible to believe that many of the problems that face our present-day church structures are a direct result of this total domination by men—and by men who did not have the slightest conception of what a woman is or how she reacts. If the woman was suppressed and repressed in Nazi Germany, she certainly suffered the same fate from the men who ruled her in Christian society. The greatest contribution that she can offer us is her capacity for love. Perhaps if she had been included as an equal, our churches would never have become involved with buildings and structures and material things. Instead, she would have constantly reminded us that the basic function of Christian churches is to teach men how to love one another.

It is entirely possible that the male-dominated church structures killed love rather than helped it to grow. It is a fact that until very recently, all of the churches regarded woman as a sort of "human breeding factory." She was to submit to sexual intercourse whenever the man decided she should, and get pregnant at his inclination. The churches restricted her activities to being the "heart of the home." Less than ten years ago, I saw an article in a religious paper that insisted that, for her, sex is a "sacred marital duty." What a distortion of the love that God built into sexuality! Just how much love was the "good church woman" of the past able to share with her husband and children?

Many of you who read these thoughts are going to feel that I have been unnecessarily hard on the men. In twentieth-century America, many men feel that women are taking over the world and that our society is female-dominated, rather than male-dominated. It is possible that we could move in this direction. Many women have rebelled against the suppression of the past; many homes are dominated by women who insist that they are not going to live as their mother had to live. I think that you are all aware, too, that when a woman is in a position of complete and unquestioned authority in a home, she becomes just as arrogant and unbearable as a man in the same position. When one person is totally dominated by another, the element of respect is lacking.

In the last few chapters, we talked about understanding and communications. Perhaps many of you have not really started to communicate yet in the discussion period in your classroom. This is not hard to understand because your experiences in the past with communications may not have been too good, and there has been very little opportunity for you to sit down and discuss things that really matter to you with people of the other sex. I hope that, today, this communication will really open and that through this you will begin to understand that these sometimes mysterious people are not very different from yourselves.

Even the phrase "opposite sex" is not good. Men and women just are not opposites. A boy and a girl from the same family and the same general kind of background probably think and feel much more alike than two girls from two entirely different backgrounds. There are a great many differences between men and women, of course, and most of them are obvious and enjoyable. But they are not opposites; they are complementary. In every sense of the term, a woman complements a man and a man complements a woman.

It is a little foolish to try to define exactly the differences between men and women at the present time. We know so little about the subject. We have had so many centuries of complete separation of the sexes and poor communications between the sexes that we really have no idea of whether the differences between men and women are genuine or merely cultural.

The masculine and feminine trap is an easy one to wander into. I wandered into it. In our original *Marriage Enrichment Program*, in a record called "Men and Women Are Different," I pointed to the woman as a full-time lover and said that she was fully absorbed in the love of her husband and family. She achieved a mature sexuality only when she first received a mature love from her husband. The man we said was a different kind of person and love was less important to him. The male ego was only completed in a mature sexuality and he only loved in a mature fashion as a result of a mature sexual relationship.

The majority of people really liked and still do like this presentation simply because it seems obvious that most women are far more concerned with love than men are. It seems obvious, too, that men are far more concerned with sex than women are. But there always were the 10 percent of the men and women who were dissatisfied with this description. Are men and women really that much different, or are most of us simply trained to be that way? This is the thing that I think you are going to want to explore in your discussions, because your generation is going to have to discover the real meaning of being masculine and being feminine. We do not know what to tell you—and those of us who pretend that we do are being foolish. To aid you in the discovery of what kind of people you really are, perhaps we can cite some examples that point out that men and women are a lot more alike than they are different.

Down through the centuries, frigidity has always been called a "woman's problem." Webster defines frigidity as "being without warmth of feeling or manner," but the way that it is usually used in marriage manuals is that the *woman* is sexually cold and unreceptive to sexual intercourse. If there were problems with sexual relations in marriage, it must have been the woman's fault because men have no problems with this. Man is a sexual aggressor; he is instantly ready for sexual relations and he knows all about it.

In your class discussions, you may have already found out how deep-rooted this myth is. When you got into the sexual area, you probably discovered that the young women in the class were willing to learn and question; however, the young men in the class felt that they had to act bored and unconcerned as if this were all "old stuff" to them and they knew all about it. Several thousands of years of conditioning that men have no problems with sex has gotten these men just as hung-up on male competency in sex as their fathers before them. You young men may want to think about this, and perhaps you will even try being honest in your discussions.

While it is true that a large percentage of women turn sexually cold in marriage, frigidity is seldom just the woman's problem. It is usually a problem of the relationship between the man and the woman—a complete misunderstanding on the part of the husband of the things that she needs. Women are not frigid; they are simply misunderstood and mishandled. We will be discussing this misunderstanding more in the next chapter.

If we want to define frigidity as "being incapable of adequately performing the sex act," the American male is probably far more frigid than the American female. Because of a complete misunderstanding of themselves and their partner, a huge percentage of American males come to their climax in sexual intercourse long before the wife is ready to respond. In addition, in the past few years there has been a vast increase in the number of males who suffer from impotency; they are unable to have an erection when it is needed for sexual intercourse.

There seem to be few physical reasons for frigidity in either the man or the woman. Many medical people feel that physical frigidity is so rare that it only occurs because of a severe accident or birth defect that cripples the genital organs. If we want to discover the reasons behind frigidity and impotency in marriage, we have to look beyond the physical aspects to the relationship between the man and the woman and to the things they have been taught about their own and their partner's sexuality.

If we want to talk about temporary impotency—the man and the woman being psychologically unable to perform the sexual act enjoyably—we would probably have to include almost 100 percent of all married couples. Again, this is related to how we feel about sex and how we feel about ourselves and about each other. In other words, it is related to what we are as people—and we are very much alike.

Impotency and frigidity begin in childhood for both men and women through the ignorance, superstition, and fear with which the sexual act is often surrounded. Perhaps the worst of these superstitions is the concept that sex is wrong and sinful because it is the animal part of us expressing itself, and we cannot let the animal take charge.

Psychologically, of course, the sexual relationship has to be a loving kind of relationship with *both* the man and the woman. If either one feels that he is being used or in any way forced into the sexual act, they will respond with some form of frigidity or impotency.

Our old formula that the woman needs love before she can respond with a mature sexuality is certainly true. Unfortunately, in marriage, the situation in the average couple's bedroom often resembles rape rather than love because husbands are completely unaware of their wife's need for love.

But it is equally true that no man can develop a satisfying and mature sexual relationship unless he is first loved. He can perform the act of sexual intercourse, of course, without love. But so can she. This kind of physical act simply consists of a little excitement and a relieving of the pressure on the male. It is very frustrating to both of them, and it is not even remotely related to mature love-making.

different. To point up the very necessary idea that no woman can respond with mature sexuality unless she is surrounded by love, her "femininity" and "delicacy" is sometimes overstressed. To convey this impression, they make a great deal of the idea that women are soft and rounded—a natural receptacle for love. This must be a little hard on a woman whom nature has constructed hard and angular but who may be an even more perfect receptacle for love.

In contrast to this oversimplified approach, many outstanding biologists are almost reverent in their expression of the very small physical differences that determine whether a person will be male or female. Many of the sex organs are almost exactly the same; many of the hormones that determine sexuality are almost the same.

Yet with all of these similarities between the sexes, it still remains true that, at the present time, most women are more deeply engrossed in love than most men are. Perhaps it is our rearing, our training, or our conditioning. Perhaps the capacity to love and to express real feelings has been bred out of men by a society that will not let him cry when hurt or express his real feelings. Perhaps the woman's need for protection has been exaggerated in a society which has insisted that the feminine half of the human race is largely incompetent and irrational. At any rate, any man who hopes to have a successful marriage has to be aware of his wife's constant and deep-seated need for affection, attention, and respect.

For whatever the reason, it is equally true that most men in today's society do have more diversified interests than women. As a matter of fact, they tend to forget all about her when they get absorbed in their work or even a football game on Sunday afternoon. Again, this is a fact about which any successful married woman will have to keep reminding herself.

Probably most women are more practical than their husbands. They tend to be more concerned with the *here* and *now* and how it affects the people whom they love. Many men tend to be more visionary and think of long-range solutions, rather than the things that women see as important today. Men generally are more involved in politics and movements and abstract ideas, while most women are more concerned about how all of these things affect their family.

It is certainly true that a majority of women are more person-centered, while men tend to think in terms of things. It is very hard for a woman to understand, for example, that a man can be angry or upset at his boss or his work or his schooling; and it is especially hard for her to understand how he can be upset about something that happened in Europe or India. When he's worried or upset, the farthest thing from his mind might be his relationship to her. Yet the first thought in her mind might be, "Now what did I do wrong? He does not love me anymore."

Certainly, the average woman is much tougher emotionally than a man. There doesn't seem to be any question about this when we look at the statistics on

conflicts fit many people. Certainly husbands and wives can derive a great deal of benefit by listening to it and talking about it.

But as the world advances and progresses and women achieve the respect they have always deserved, it will be far more useful to think of marriage as an intense relationship between two entirely different people, with totally different backgrounds. It is only when we try to understand and respect this other *person* that we begin to find ourselves truly complementing each other.

DISCUSS

Classroom Discussion. From your observations and the things that you have said to each other during the past several weeks, all of you will have formed some opinions as to what mature masculinity and mature femininity means. I hope that you will not restrict this discussion to any set formula or rules. Probably several of the girls in class can talk about what being a woman means to them and several boys can discuss manliness.

If you are sincere in using this program to become better people, you will certainly want to discuss how young people sometimes can hurt the so-called effeminate boy and the masculine girl. And probe a great deal deeper into the meaning of masculinity and femininity—more than big busts and big shoulders. Just for fun, you might try to organize a whole debate around the words "masculine" and feminine" to see if you can arrive at any single trait that always means that a person is masculine or one that always means that a person is feminine. I think you may be surprised at the results.

Discussion at Home. This discussion should prove to be one of the most interesting ones to report to your parents. In the world that most of them grew up in, the words masculine and feminine were clearly defined, even if the definitions were none too accurate. One of the toughest parts of their marriage was to discover each other as persons. Many young people compare their dads and their mothers against other dads and mothers. In your discussion, you may want to ask yourself if you have been fair to them in doing this or whether you should have thought of them as individuals.

4. *Respect for the sexuality of the person.* He has discarded the "hurting" concepts of sex and accepts it as an important part of the total personality.

OBSERVE III

Observe yourself. We are drawing close to the end of the program, and this is a time to concentrate on a realistic self-appraisal. What kind of sexual maturity have you been able to achieve? It would be surprising if you still did not have a great many doubts and fears about yourself as a sexual person. I hope you have observed that nearly all of your classmates have the same doubts and fears. You can best help yourselves by sharing your feelings. We grow as people as we help other people to grow.

Sexuality reflects
the total life of man

Many times throughout this program, we have said that a mature sexuality is the sum total of everything that you are as a person. In a very real sense, each act of sexual intercourse will be the climax of all of the love that you have received and all of the love that you have given up to the point of the act itself. It is the sum total of what you are: your communications, your prayers, your understanding, your feelings, and your emotions that are expressed finally in the physical act of love-making. If the sum total of these things is good, then your love-making will be good; if it is bad, your purely physical act will be destructive.

We have seen, too, that all of our physical relations are not only determined by the kind of life that we have led, but that they also influence the life that we lead. Loving sexual relations makes all of us better people, and no marriage can succeed without deep and loving sexual relations. The "ideal" that was posed by some far-out religious leaders of years ago of husband and wife living together as brother and sister is sheer nonsense. Unless we are lovers in every meaning of the term, no real marriage can exist.

Sexual intercourse is the climax of all of the love that we put into our marriage, and an ideal marriage is one in which we spend all of our lives preparing

and goodness that has to be a part of every loving relationship.

On the part of most women, this may mean a complete change in attitude from those they have brought into marriage. It would be very surprising if most girls did not pick up some fears or some feelings that this is a kind of "necessary evil," or even that it is a thing that people do because they are part animal. These attitudes are a sharp contrast to the real dignity built into the sexual act of God and the beauty with which it must be surrounded if it is to become a healthy, vital thing.

The only person who can continuously supply this sense of beauty to the woman is her husband. Yet many men utterly destroy the capacity of their wife to love simply by how they approach her. Some men use "gutter language" and treat their wives like a prostitute. Some men are brutal in the sexual act and some even forget the personal little things like cleanliness, privacy, and patience that every woman needs before she can accept sexual relations with joy.

3. *The physical preparation of the woman.* Far too much has been made of this preparation in the past. Unnatural stress is still put on the physical preparation by the little minds who somehow equate a woman to a washing machine that has to be adjusted before it will function adequately. Her physical preparation is important, but it is a natural outgrowth of the love that her husband has for her. As he loves her, he wants to totally possess her and when he does, he naturally fondles her breasts and her vagina; in the process, he brings her to the point of readiness.

Only two things are physically necessary for her readiness for sexual intercourse. The first of these is that the vagina be completely lubricated. Since sex is much more of a mental thing than it is a physical one, this process of lubrication actually starts a long time before a man and a woman are in bed together. It is completed with his touching the clitoris, which is a small penis-like organ that is highly sensitive and lies at the top of the vagina, and the tips of the breasts which are also highly sensitive sexual triggers.

The other important part of her physical preparation is that love-making be continued until she reaches the point at which she desires to receive the penis of the man. In most marriages, this does not happen; the man initiates sexual intercourse. Here again, the reason does not lie in anything physical. It simply happens this way because we have believed for so long in the supremacy of the male and the idea of the man being a sexual aggressor that almost everyone has believed that he should initiate intercourse. Yet nearly all of the problems that the man experiences with ejaculating too soon can be eliminated by waiting until she is completely ready.

Perhaps even more important to mention in a program of this type, is the complete preparation of the man. Because of the superstitions surrounding male superiority in sex, many people are totally unaware of the fact that the man has to be prepared at all. This widespread belief is probably responsible for more sexual failure in marriage than for any other one thing. People do not fail in marriage because they do not

Perhaps the basic idea of mature love, mature sexuality, mature marriage and just plain mature living, is beginning to emerge now. Before we can discover happiness anywhere, we have to grow up ourselves as far as it is possible to do so. If a woman wants to have a real man for her husband, she has to build that man all through her life. If a man wants to have a grown-up woman for a wife, he has to build her all through his life. Love is a life-long process of building love and the capacity to love in ourselves and in each other. It is a creating kind of thing, rather than a receiving kind of thing.

2. *The spiritual preparation of the man.* Men, too, have to be prepared spiritually for sexual intercourse. Unfortunately, in today's world, this means that most men will have to undertake a total re-examination of their basic beliefs. When most men get married, their sexual convictions are generally a mixture of over-confidence in their so-called masculinity, fears that they might not be adequate, superstition, and just plain old "gutter" information that has nothing whatsoever to do with mature sex. If the man loves his wife, he will want to surround every loving act with the beauty and dignity that she needs to be fulfilled. This is not easy if he carries into marriage the idea that sex is a place in which he must "prove" his masculinity. The only "proof" that a woman needs is that this is a loving act. People who need to use each other sexually to prove themselves are many light years away from the maturity that is needed to make marriage and sexual relations succeed.

Many ideas about sex that we pick up from other men are "hurting" and "proving." Deep penetration of the penis is one of them. Violence in the sex act is another. The "hickey" idea is a third. None of them has anything to do with the pleasure and joy of sex. As a matter of fact, most of them destroy the woman's ability to respond.

The fact that a "real man" can have sexual intercourse several times a night is another of our hurting "tavern information" concepts. Just about any young man can —if he doesn't love his wife and doesn't care about a loving relationship. Nothing can turn a woman sour on sex as quickly as the feeling that she is being used. Some place along the line, every young man is going to have to ask himself the questions: "What is this really all about?" and "What kind of marriage do I want?" I suppose that there is a certain kind of satisfaction for a certain kind of weak little man in conquering or subduing his wife. But there can be no real happiness for any man who does not have a deep and lasting respect for sexual love, and consideration for the woman who loves him.

3. *The physical preparation of the man.* The physical preparation of the man is again a natural result of the woman's love for him. Because she cares for all of him as a person, she wants to possess all of him. As she does, she rather naturally and lovingly caresses the base of the penis and testicles. When she does this, a little semen, which ordinarily does not contain sperm, is given off from the end of the penis. This relaxes the

It means that if the husband does climax before the wife is ready, he will continue the love-making until she is satisfied and can comfortably relax.

It means that they approach sex with a great deal of humor—they learn to laugh a little together at the days when it does not work very well, instead of blaming themselves and each other.

We have said many times before that sex is for adults. It is. The *doing* part of sex is very simple, and any child who has reached puberty can do it. But the *being* part of sex is a lot more difficult.

DISCUSS

Classroom Discussion. Some of you may have read a great deal in the area of sexuality. Many of the things that you've read may seem to contradict the concepts that we are speaking about throughout this book. Through your reading and through your experiences, you may have even developed some strong convictions about sexual freedom, the new morality, and the techniques and mechanics of sexual relations.

This is good. We have said consistently through this course that you are young adults, and that the decisions you make regarding yourself as a person, regarding sexuality, and your relationships with other people are your own to make. However, it is just as wrong to sit back and to smugly assume that you have all the answers, as it is to blandly agree with everything that is said. The place to test your ideas is right here, in this classroom, with other people who are just as concerned and just as knowledgeable about the components of a mature sexuality as you are. Get your ideas out in the open, and talk about them. Don't be afraid to defend them if they seem right to you. If you've been doing your homework and participating in the discussion, you probably are far too honest with yourself by now to persist in an argument simply for the sake of winning it.

Set your own agenda for this discussion on a mature sexuality. There is very little that we can do at this point to guide you. Few, if any, adults of this generation have had the opportunity to delve into their own feelings and the feelings of the people around them that you have had during the course of this program. Since the experience is just as new to us as it is to you, we have no idea where your discussion will be at this point. We hope that you have been able to achieve an openness and honesty that we've not been able to achieve in our lifetimes.

Discussion at Home. You will want to keep constantly in mind that everyone wants to communicate openly. Your parents do, too. But in some cases, their early experiences with communication have been so bad that it still may be difficult for them. They will need your constant encouragement. The more free that you become in telling them what is happening to you, the more possible it becomes for them to relax and talk things over with you.

Young people need to keep in mind that it is impossible to change people, advise people, or to force people to become what you want them to become. This applies

serving these families, so that you can attempt to discuss them intelligently later:

1. Do the families that you are observing appear to have been planned? Did they just happen? How have the children responded to the size of the family? How has it affected the love relationship between the parents and between the parents and children?

2. Have you observed any relationship between the size of the family and the mental health and stability of the people involved in it?

3. Do you think that more children or less children would have made a difference in these families?

4. Does there seem to be a difference in feeling between one child and another child?

5. If you have become comfortable enough to talk to the people you're observing, how do they say they feel about family size? When do they think that couples should have children?

Planning is a
personal thing

Along with the growth of family life education, we are finally beginning to recognize our responsibility to give some serious thought to the size of the family that we will have and to the rights of the children that we will bring into the world. The old idea, which was a strong part of our religious background, was that the "Lord will provide." Probably this worked very well during the time that most people lived on farms and an extra child was another hand to help with the chores.

With the growth of the cities and most people working in industries, many Protestant ministers began talking about the fact that the size of the family was the responsibility of the husband and wife. Catholics followed later with the clear statement on family planning by the Vatican Council. Nearly every thinking person today agrees that families should be planned and that the responsibility of planning rests with the parents.

Like all areas that are even remotely associated with human sexuality, the whole subject of family planning is clouded by myths, superstitions, and misinformation. An example of this is the two extremes that we still read about today. One is the panic reaction of certain sociologists and population experts who insist that soon there will be standing room only on this earth of ours and suggest that in the future, we will have to receive govern-

example is that of the young couple who get married because the girl is pregnant. In most cases, these couples are far too immature to be able to accept the responsibility of really loving one another. They simply compound one mistake with a far more serious one. Most men and women have a great deal of trouble accepting and loving a child who appears when they are not ready for him. As we have pointed out in Chapter V, the feeling part of us is largely built into our bodies and is very difficult to control. In nearly every home of the last generation, both the woman and the man had as many different feelings about their children as they had children. This is natural and, perhaps, inevitable.

Let us look at what happens to the feeling part of the husband and wife when children appear. Perhaps the first pregnancy came as a complete surprise to both of them; neither of them were in any way ready for it. They may have been quarreling and bickering constantly when the pregnancy occurred. Immediately the woman has the fear, "Will my husband even be around when this child arrives?" Perhaps the husband is so immature that he is ashamed of his wife and won't take her out in public as she gets bigger and approaches the birth of her child.

How are the mother and father going to feel about this particular child? With their minds, they are going to love him, of course. But, how about the feeling part? Aren't they always going to feel somewhat uncomfortable with this child?

In a real sense, each child is born into a different family. Some come into the family because they are wanted by both the husband and the wife, and both have looked forward to him with happy expectancy. Some children are born when the family already has more children than they can cope with, and the parents are actually afraid of the child when it appears. Wouldn't it be better if people only had children that they wanted and needed because their love demanded it?

Family planning is certainly a subject that the young couple will want to talk about a great deal before marriage and all through their marriage. Circumstances are constantly changing, and readiness for children is constantly changing. The problem of how to limit children is a difficult one, and one that most couples do not solve easily. Simply selecting a reliable method of controlling birth and sticking to this method without really talking it through can be an extremely destructive thing.

In a relatively few cases, the couple may be mature enough and love each other and their children enough to let children come as they want to come through all of their married life. Strangely enough, some couples who do not practice any method of birth control at all do not seem to have too many children. The studies that we are currently completing at the Family Life Bureau indicate, for example, that couples who do not use any method of birth control have fewer children than couples who use the rhythm system.

For the vast majority of couples, however, some method of family planning, acceptable to both of them, helps to increase their love for both each other and their children. To aid in your discussion of this area,

structive to the relationship of the man and the woman. There is also the question of what happens to the people if they ever change their minds and desire children.

2. *Barrier methods.* These are methods that keep the sperm of the man from reaching the ovum of the woman. Under this category, we can put the condom, the diaphragm, cervical cap, and jelly and foam preparations that block the mouth of the uterus and prevent the sperm from penetrating. Your library will give you detailed information on all of these methods.

Our studies indicate that the effectiveness of these methods varies a great deal from person to person. All of them require care in their use, and the person who is careless in following directions may find the best of these methods ineffective. As with all methods of contraception, if the couple does not have trust and confidence in the one that they choose, there is a fear of pregnancy which distracts from the pleasure that they are able to give each other.

Some people tell us that they find one or the other of these barrier methods very satisfying and dependable. However, many others feel that they destroy the spontaneous effect of sexual intercourse. In every case, some sort of preparation is needed shortly before love-making. Having to interrupt to insert a diaphragm, jellies, or to place a condom over the penis can cause the excitement level to go down. Many people's feelings are even stronger than this; the whole process disgusts them. This is especially true with people who have been brought up to believe that sexual intercourse is a little bit wrong anyway.

3. *Spermicidals and douches.* The purpose of these is to destroy the male sperm after sexual intercourse. These are not generally used today and are seldom recommended by a physician. Many of them are not reliable and some can actually cause damage to the woman.

4. *Cyclic methods.* These are often mis-called "natural" methods of birth control. They all make some attempt to discover when the woman ovulates and then suggest that the couple refrain from sexual intercourse for several days prior to and after ovulation. Included in this category are the calendar rhythm method, the basal temperature method, and various devices placed within the vagina to determine the time of ovulation. Its advocates suggest that it can be highly effective "when used with well-motivated couples," that sexual relations are natural (no device interferes with the act), and that the discipline of using this method increases the love between the couple.

But the cyclic methods are being intensely scrutinized at the present time within the Catholic church. Certain facts are becoming increasingly evident: a. With a vast majority of people, these are *not* birth control methods. A very large percentage of people who consistently practice one of the rhythm methods have more children than people who use no method at all. b. Responses on our own questionnaires, as well as those of other researchers, indicate that this method is extremely destructive to the relationship. People simply cannot make love by the calendar. c. The morality of the cyclic methods is being questioned. It may be quite immoral; children are frequently unexpected and unwanted. The love of the couple may be severely damaged; and most women, in particular, have constant fear of pregnancy, which is again destructive to sexual harmony and communications in the home.

A great deal has been written recently about this system. A couple who is contemplating marriage would do well to do some extensive reading before deciding that rhythm is their only possibility.

5. *Intrauterine devices* (*IUD*). These are devices that are inserted into the uterus of the female to prevent the fertile egg from developing. Generally, these are very inexpensive and are used extensively in underdeveloped countries. Their advantage is that they are highly reliable and are not associated with the act of sexual intercourse. The disadvantage is that the intrauterine device has to be inserted by a medical doctor. Some women experience bleeding, and some experience pain. In some cases, the device is passed while urinating without the woman's being aware of it.

6. *The "pill."* This is perhaps the most promising of the family planning methods. In its present development, the various kinds of birth control pills are taken regularly over a period of time. They contain hormones that are similar to those that the body normally secretes during pregnancy. Their reaction in the body is quite complicated, and medical people are not fully in agreement on just how they work and on what the side effects may be. However, the pill has been used very extensively in modern America, as well as many foreign countries; it has been approved by the Food and Drug Administration, and the side effects experienced have

been relatively low. It has several great advantages over all other methods of birth control. The first of these is that it may be close to 100% effective when used responsibly. There seems to be increasing evidence that pregnancy results only when the woman has forgotten to take the pill or when she has used the pill without medical guidance or an understanding of its use.

A second great advantage of the pill is that it is not directly related to sexual intercourse. There is no feeling of something having to be done immediately before or after sexual intercourse.

Finally, the pill has many other medically useful qualities besides the prevention of conception. It can be used to correct hormone imbalance, many menstrual problems, and is quite useful in modifying the changes that occur in middle-aged women during menopause.

Disadvantages include some uncertainty of the side effects and the fact that it does require some discipline on the part of the woman taking them. The pill is also quite expensive in comparison to some of the other methods of birth control.

The reason that the pill seems so promising is that it is highly effective and still developing. In the very near future, for example, there may be a "morning after" pill that can be taken after intercourse; a pill that will actually pinpoint ovulation; and a pill that will give protection to the woman for long periods of time. Even a pill that can be taken by the man is a possibility. It is conceivable that developments in this area will eventually solve the old Catholic-Protestant controversy on birth control and provide a method that is satisfying to both.

For the present, however, the matter of choosing an acceptable method of birth control is still not a simple one. It is very difficult for the Catholic, for example, who has been raised all of his life to believe that any method of birth control is definitely wrong, to accept the fact that he has to make his own decision on this and that he will be responsible for the decision. There is increasing evidence that more reactions to the pill occur in Catholic women, and that some of these may be largely psychological.

For all men and women who have decisions to make regarding birth control, the basic problem remains one of communication. There is no one method that is completely acceptable to all people. If couples are not really talking things over in other areas, they can make their life miserable by continuing a practice that is hateful to one or the other of them.

In the past, the whole area of birth control has been surrounded by far too much guilt. Even today, there are a lot of people who seem determined to make us feel guilty about the choices that we make. There are those who would tell us that anyone who has more than one child or two is completely irresponsible. There are those who tell us that every child must have a college education and that we have to give it to them. Finally, there are those who insist that we have to practice rhythm, even though all responsible evidence indicates that few couples can find this a workable solution.

It is becoming increasingly important to recognize that this is *our* home, *our* life, and that these will be *our* children, and *we* are responsible for them. The persons who will ultimately have to answer for their child-bearing decisions are the man and the woman who have given birth to these children.

When Jeanette and I reach this day of judgment, we feel very strongly that the primary thing that we will have to answer for in our family is love. We feel that the questions He will be most concerned about are these: "What kind of love did you give to each other?" "What kind of love did you show your children?" "What kind of love did your family help to produce in the world that I created?"

DISCUSS

Classroom Discussion. It will, again, be difficult to guide the maturity of your discussion in the area of family planning. You will not be trying, of course, to decide how many children you're going to have or the method that you will use to achieve a planned or unplanned family. These decisions will have to be reached someday with the person whom you will marry, and they will have to be discussed again and again all through your lives. Medical technology is advancing so quickly that it is not even possible to anticipate the methods of family planning that may be available to you several years from now. The important thing is that you open up your thinking about this area. It is important, too, that you go into marriage with considerably more knowledge than it was possible to get in the brief chapter that you have just finished. It's *your* class, and *your* discussion. You may even want to bring in a doctor or one or several clergymen to give you a great deal more information about the subject before you even begin your discussion.

I hope that you will not become entirely "practical" in your discussion on family planning. Family planning is just another tool to build a love relationship in the home. Fitting family planning into this building of love has to be your prime consideration.

Discussion in the Home. Perhaps your parents will feel free enough by now to talk to you about family planning. Their experiences can be very valuable to you. Hopefully, they will not only discuss what they have done about family planning, but will also discuss what they wish they had done about it in the past.

Chapter XII

The Practical Part of Marriage

OBSERVE

UP UNTIL NOW, YOU HAVE BEEN DEALING WITH PEOPLE and relationships between people. By far the best way to discover the act of getting along with people is by practicing it and by observing people who are getting along with each other. But for the first part of this chapter, we are dealing with a thing; and this *thing* is the handling of finance in marriage. It's a thing that many of you may not have very much knowledge about. If you start your conversations on finance simply by reading the chapter and the few things that you might observe in your home, there's a very great chance that you'll be talking from ignorance. You have a decision to make at this point. Do you want to find out more about the financial aspects of marriage? If you do, you've got some homework to do.

In your town are a great many people who know a lot about money and handling the family budget. They include bankers, credit union managers, home economists, insurance men, and attorneys. Most of these people will be willing to talk to your class if you want them to. It's important to keep in mind, however, that every one of them has something to sell. The banker will naturally be prejudiced toward borrowing money from banks; the credit union manager, from a credit union; the department store manager, an easy-payment plan. The facts that they present may be somewhat "colored," even though they have no intention of deliberately deceiving you. It will be up to you to question them thoroughly, and come up with a balanced idea of what finance is all about.

I would suggest that you strongly consider inviting these specialists in. It will be a welcome relief from your concentrated observation of the same people and should lay the groundwork for an interesting and lively discussion.

OBSERVE II

The idea of "doing your own thing" is an important one that you're probably going to have to do your homework on. Carefully observe your couples and see how they feel about the work that they are doing. From this, you can decide just how much this feeling affects their family life at home.

Working out
the details together

In the past eleven chapters, we have been talking about sex and love and all kinds of interesting things that fascinate adults of all ages. It has probably been an exciting program. Now suddenly we descend into something that is drab and unexciting. For the next few days, we will be reading and talking about the practical part of marriage.

Yet these common, simple everyday things that we are going to be discussing here are the things that make your sexuality and love function. Beauty in love only exists in a real world; and unless the young couple pays some attention to the practical aspects of marriage, they will be so overwhelmed by them that there just won't be any time for love.

Again, this chapter does not intend to go into any great detail in any of the areas that we cover. Its main purpose is to start you thinking, reading, and talking about them so that you will come up with some workable solutions of your own. It is a sort of smorgasbord of common sense that follows the same principles that we have been stressing all through this program: communication, understanding, and acceptance. If you follow this simple approach in your marriage, solving the practical problems will be much easier than if you decide that you are going to do it your way, not your partner's way. Nearly every new family is blessed with a person who is far more practical than his [or her] mate. If you approach the whole area with an open mind, it will be easier to discover who that person is.

It always amuses me in marriage counseling to watch a highly impractical, visionary person operate. Strangely, this is the one who insists on handling the money and in doing so, oversees most of the practical decisions. What he really needs is a guardian. Even in the rare home in which neither of the individuals is very practical, solutions can be worked out with the two of them really communicating.

The first practical item that causes a lot of difficulty in a lot of homes is handling the money. This is a money-oriented world. With television and radio, someone is trying to sell us something almost every waking hour of the day; and this is good. In modern-day America, we can almost think of spending money as a kind of charity. The money that we spend provides people with jobs, pride and dignity.

Let's take that new car that you want to buy sometime as an example. When you buy that car, you probably go to the bank and pay them interest on it. The money that you pay keeps additional people working at the bank. The car dealer has a family to support, and he employs a lot of people whom he could not employ if you and all of us did not buy cars. He, in turn, buys the car from the factory, which again, employs all kinds of people.

The money that you spend is a good and useful thing —if you spend it responsibly, if the things that you buy serve to increase your love, rather than putting strain and worry on your marriage that makes you nervous and irritable and hard on each other.

Unfortunately, most young couples have too many things that they "need." The people who are trying to sell you these things are often sincere people, and they really believe that you do need them. Yet many young couples ruin any chance that their marriage has for success by plunging themselves badly in debt to purchase things that really were not needed at all. I have personally encountered new couples with no children who have enough pots and pans to cook for a family of twelve, because someone convinced them that they needed them now. There are probably millions of young couples with a brand new baby who own four- or five-hundred dollars worth of children's books. There is no question that these are wonderful things for children; but the unfortunate thing is that by the time the child gets old enough to read, the books will be outdated.

The insurance man who comes to your door is deeply sincere when he tells you that every young home needs large quantities of life insurance, liability insurance, home-owner's insurance, burglary insurance, and that every parent should certainly take out an endowment fund for the children who will later go to college. He is right; we all should have these things—if we can afford them. When we meet these sincere and honest people who tell us what we need, it is often very hard to remember that our prime responsibility is to give each other love and that a part of this giving is to keep each other free from financial strain.

Nearly every young marriage is short of money and this, too, is good. If they don't learn financial responsibility now, they probably never will learn it. This is why it is necessary to talk things over fully and honestly. Their needs are so great at that time. Most young people have been short of money all of their lives and have always been looking forward to the day when they could get rid of the old "wreck" of a car that they own, the cast-off clothing that they have been forced to wear, and buy the things that they want. In some cases, these needs are overwhelming. The surprising thing that we see in the Negro and Spanish ghettos, for example, is that when they start working, the men may buy a diamond ring or a huge automobile that they could never have afforded before. They buy it because they have never felt like anyone and now they want to show people that they really are someone.

If we are married to a person like this, we simply cannot make these needs go away by refusing to recognize them. It takes a great deal of talking to begin to understand them, and sometimes it may be worthwhile for the young family to delay buying something "practical" and spend the money on something "unpractical" simply because they need it.

All of us are extremely vulnerable where our children are concerned. We want them to have many of the things that we never had: college education, outboard motors, snow machines, new bicycles, etc. Yet, if you will look at the experiences in your own home, you will quickly recognize that *things* were not the basic ingredient of happiness. What were the things that you really wanted from your parents? Wasn't it more of their attention and love?

Along with the sincere, legitimate enterprisers, we have a few advertising quacks who try to use your love to force you to buy things for each other. I like to call these people "fear merchants" because this is what they are. They are using all of our insecurity and our feelings "that nobody could really love me" to force us to buy love. These people even hire psychologists to discover our feelings and insecurities. They indicate that "she won't love you" unless we buy her enough life insurance to make sure that she never has to work a day in her life, a sexy car, or even the right type of body deodorant. When we are afraid that our wives or husbands don't love us, we could save a lot of money by merely asking them or by simply giving ourselves to them. The idea of getting love or attention through things alone is ridiculous.

It is a great temptation to go into the whole area of finance. We could talk about budgeting; about interest rates; about time purchases; about how much of your income should be spent on food, clothing, and rent; about insurance needs; in other words, about every area of money-handling that affects a young marriage. If we did, however, we would have a whole book just on finance. Perhaps the only important thing that we can say here is that this *is* a very important part of marriage, and part of maturity is financial maturity. Every young couple will want to spend a great deal of time reading widely and discussing the area of finance with responsible people.

Perhaps the most helpful suggestion that we can make is that you face your finances immediately; that every payday you talk about your finances; that you always know exactly what you owe and what you earn. The majority of the problems that we see are problems that have been created by people who just keep buying without any real idea of what their financial situation is. Again, sound financing is just a small part of the total pattern of responsible behavior: of accepting responsibility for the things that we do. And money is only one of the practical problems that we have to work through in order for our marriage to grow.

Perhaps one of the things that is even more important than money is the work that you will do to support your family. This is sometimes called your vocation. Probably no one particular thing has a greater effect on how people feel and how they act toward each other in marriage than the work that they do.

There tends to be a great deal of panic about this in the world today. Almost from the time a young man falls out of the cradle, someone is telling him, "You'd better decide what your vocation in life will be." Sometimes high school guidance counselors tend to get a little carried away with this and expect a young person to make his decision, as a freshman or sophomore in high school, without any knowledge on which to base his decision. This is nonsense and completely contrary to what we know about the individual. A simple survey of successful men will show you that most of them had no idea what their eventual career would be when they were your age. Most of these men experimented with a number of different vocations before they found one that they really liked and wanted to settle down in. It is true that quite early in our lives, we may have to make a decision as to whether we are going to work with our hands or work with our minds. Even this can be a bad decision because many people's mental capacity does not start to function in certain areas until well beyond the high school years. But in the present educational system, it is a decision that most young people have to make. If they go in the direction of the mechanical skills, they will probably be missing the courses that they will need for college; and if they take the college-preparation courses, they probably will be missing the mechanical skill courses that they will need to get a job in this field.

One of the Puritan ideas that we seem to be stuck with in this country is the idea that we have to get a job and stick to it. If we do this, we are considered steady and reliable. Yet, we may be miserably unhappy and the misery that we create by doing something that we hate often carries over to our partners.

As I have mentioned before, I really like the "hippie" slogan, "Do your own thing." People who are working at jobs that they really enjoy find it much easier to carry over their happiness and contentment into the home. I see this "Do your own thing" as really being in keeping with the way that God has created us. All of us have an entirely different background and different experiences. These experiences create a temperament that is different from anyone else's. They prepare every one of us for a certain, specific task that we can do better than anyone else can. It hardly seems possible that we can find this separate little niche without some searching. A person who can decide during high school what he is going to be for the rest of his life and then carry through on this decision happily and contentedly is a rare exception.

When we are talking about women, we really have some hang-ups on vocation. We tend to say things like, "either she will be a professional person or a housewife," as if these were two separate things and incompatible with each other. This idea of the woman being an "either-or" kind of being has really hurt us and has been especially destructive to the love relationship of a man and woman in marriage.

Most women have to have something that they are deeply interested in besides their husband and children if they are going to keep on loving them. Letting a woman's mind stagnate on baby-talk for twenty years or more while her children are in the home is extremely damaging. Suddenly she finds that her children are grown, and the mind that she was once so proud of has slept for twenty years, and she cannot wake it up again. A woman has to discover her unique self, the thing that she loves to do and can do better than anyone else. She needs to spend some time at that thing all during her childbearing years.

I am sure that some of our Puritan friends are going to see this chapter as recommending that you shift from job to job irresponsibly. But this is not so. Again, there is a practical element to work, even to work that we detest. It does not make any sense to continue to do something that we hate; but it makes a great deal less sense to quit a job before we know where we are going.

A large portion of the personality problems that we face in counseling can be directly attributed to the fact that men and women are not satisfied with what they are doing. For the most part, however, this comes from the feeling that they are not doing a good job at what they are doing. In your observations you will see many men and women who are doing as little as possible on their job and are taking their employer or mate for everything that they can get. All of these people are very unhappy, and most of them are quite neurotic. Doing the best possible job that you can during the time that you work is not a question of responsibility to your employer. It is a question of your own integrity. You can only live with yourself when you feel that you are doing the best possible job that you can do.

"Do your own thing" certainly does not imply, either, that we just have to do the things that we like to do. All of us have many things that we do because we have to do them, not because we like to do them. Again, this is a part of maturity and a part of your own personal integrity.

Another very practical part of marriage is the old idea of respect for the person whom you married. We have talked a great deal about acceptance and the fact that we cannot change our partner. How can we settle the issues between us, then, when both of us feel strongly about them?

Any good marriage includes a lot of little compromises—not in what you believe, but simply because you love. The man quickly realizes that in today's world, a woman has a great need for male companionship. There are many places that she likes to go where she cannot go alone. She may be very different than you are. Perhaps she is a poet or an artist, and you have no interest whatsoever in these things. This is where compromises are needed because of love. We have to share the things that one or the other of us might like, and we have to be honest. Instead of trying to force each other to change and to become carbon copies of ourselves, we have to recognize that no kind of person is the right kind of person. Each of us was created in our own individual way, and this creation is good. As we make these little compromises and try to share the things that our partner likes, we find a great deal of enjoyment that we never anticipated or expected.

While you are thinking and talking about respect for the person, I hope that your generation completely examines the whole idea of respect for the child. In our day, child rearing has been completely overdone and overemphasized. We have been a child-centered generation with the idea that good parents are parents who are always sacrificing for their children. I hope that you young adults will recognize in your marriage that parents do not live for their children and should not live for their children. I hope that you will relax a little and live in such a way that you can really learn to love each other and *enjoy* your children.

I hope, too, that you will come to recognize that the Old Testament didn't necessarily have all of the final answers on child discipline when it said, "Spare the rod, and spoil the child." Discipline is something that always comes down from the top. Since the world began, we have created generation after generation of people who did not know how to decide for themselves because decisions were always made for them at home.

It seems to me that one of the main purposes of child-rearing is to create responsible citizens who can some-day assume their place in a responsible adult world. It is a very comfortable thing sometimes for the child to have Mother and Dad make all of his decisions for him. However, it certainly does not prepare him to make decisions himself. He suddenly finds himself out in this world.

I hope that you young people will try two things in your child rearing that have never been seriously tried before. The first is to give the child increasing responsibility all through his life and expect him to use that responsibility thoughtfully. The second is that you try to open real communications with your children and keep them open through honesty. This means that you never pretend with your children that you are something that you are not. Perhaps, then, your children will feel that you are adults whom they can depend on and talk with during their adolescent years because they know who you are.

There is one last thought on the practical part of marriage that you may want to consider now and in your discussions later with the person whom you are going to marry. This concerns starting your new life together and is a question of geography. Where should you live?

One of the best meanings of adulthood is contained in the New Testament when it suggests that you "leave your father and mother and cleave to each other." What this means to me is that you learn very early in your married life to depend on each other and to leave your parents emotionally as well as physically.

Many young marriages are irreparably damaged in the first few years by too close an association with one or the other's parents. Because Dad and Mom may not like to see you move across the country or merely to another city does not mean that you have to stay home. If you really love your parents, you will recognize that they, too, have to grow up and that hanging on to their children forever is certainly not a part of maturity.

This is a very brief review of many of the practical common sense areas that all of you will want to talk over before your marriage as well as through your marriage. It is such a short summary and so many things have been left out that its only practical value is the communication that results from it. As you talk together in class and talk with your parents and friends, I hope you will find many more of the practical things that you want to explore.

DISCUSS

Classroom Discussion. You're going to have to build your own classroom discussion on finance. I have no idea if you will decide to bring people in, or what they are going to talk about when they get there. It is important that you follow up any talks that they have given with your own discussion, so that you can analyze and weigh the things that they've said.

This might well lead to a broader discussion on honesty in business, government, and school. If it does, and if you have time, let it go. Older people who do any thinking are not very proud of the morality of the world that we are leaving you. It helps to face it as it is; perhaps, through your discussion, you may even discover some little area in which you can improve the situation. It's our world. It's going to continue to be largely phony and false and dishonest until we decide to change it.

I hope that you will be able to reserve at least another day to talk over the important area of vocation. The ideas in the chapter on "do your own thing" may be different from the ones that you've heard from most people. Take them apart and look them over.

The practical things that affect our marriage go on indefinitely and haven't even been scratched in this entire course. Such things as cooking, sewing, household organization and management, working wives, and a hundred other things that you have found to be important in your observations are all well worth talking about and discussing. It's impossible to cover all of them in one short program. We have concentrated instead on basic attitudes and the communication that is always necessary to work out these problems in the home.

Discussion at Home. Your parents can be a valuable source on the practical aspects of marriage. By this time in life, most of us who have children your age have made so many mistakes that we do have something to contribute to you. You are not going to have time to discuss all of the things that you may have liked to cover in the classroom on the practical part of marriage. Perhaps you are not even ready to discuss these things; many of them do not interest you at the present time. If you have opened the communication door with your parents, you will want to make sure that this door stays open as the end of the program approaches. You are young adults. The decisions that you make from now on will largely be your own. You may not necessarily accept your parents' advice. But you will find it well worthwhile listening to and considering.

Chapter XIII

Some Thoughts on Responsibility

OBSERVE

I IMAGINE THAT ALL OF YOU WHO HAVE BEEN THROUGH this entire program may be getting a little tired of the word *responsibility*. However, it is a word that is not going to go away, and it is going to play a very important part in your entire adult life.

Search out the adults in the couples you have been observing. Look a little deeper than a pleasing personality or a good sense of humor. See how our definition of adulthood fits each of them: An adult is "an individual who accepts responsibility for his own acts—most of the time."

One of the interesting things you may observe is how much all of us want other people to make our decisions for us. It's a real temptation for everyone to "pass the buck" up the line. Somehow we believe that we will be more "comfortable" if someone else makes our decisions for us. "They" can then accept responsibility for them; and "we" can then complain about them if we like to.

Part of your observation will be to try to discover if the people who are constantly blaming others for their acts and decisions are comfortable people. Compare them to the individuals whom you know who make their own decisions and then accept responsibility for them. I think that if you do, you will begin to get the real feel of what we are trying to say when we talk about maturity.

OBSERVE II

While it is true that maturing is a gradual process that continues over an entire lifetime, some young people grasp its meaning very early in life. Hopefully, some of the friends whom you are observing may have already developed into people who are concerned for other people, who respect other people; and, as a result, are comfortable with themselves. In your observations, try to get the feel of them, too.

OBSERVE III

Once again, in closing this course, you will want to take final stock of yourself, especially in relationship to responsibility and maturity. Some people who come from unloving backgrounds spend their lives in self-pity. They are constantly projecting their problems on other people—blaming their parents and teachers for the fact that they are as they are. Yet, some people who come from unloving backgrounds develop a great deal of maturity and concern for other people. If you look around you widely enough, you will see some of these kinds of people, too. They are beautiful people.

It's your life to live

As we move into the closing hours of this program, I am thinking about all of the different kinds of people who have been involved. People are people, and they all respond differently. Some of you have tried to talk and listen to the people around you. Some have simply read the book, and a few haven't done much of anything. For those of you who have really used this program, something very good has probably happened to you. This material is not magic. However, something good always happens when we spend a long period of time looking thoroughly at ourselves and analyzing our relations with other people.

Preaching a sermon would destroy everything that has been accomplished. Young people have been exposed to too many sermons from adults, and they have seldom had the opportunity to really think things through for themselves. Yet, all the way through, we have talked about honesty; I would be something less than honest if I did not tell you how I personally feel about some of the things that we have talked about.

Many of these thoughts will be familiar to you. But perhaps we can review some of the things that should have happened during this program. We will attempt to see how these experiences can be used throughout your lives.

First of all, I hope that nearly all of you have made a good start toward communications. For some of you, this may have come hard. You do not get rid of a lifetime of training in a few short weeks, so you may have contributed very little to the discussion in the classroom and at home. Yet, even if this is true, you have probably thought a great deal about *why* it is so hard to talk. Hopefully, you are beginning to see that it is possible to communicate better than you do—even if you have to start with a close, personal friend.

I believe quite a few of you have had some good experiences with honesty and with expressing how you feel about things. Honesty hurts; it will hurt you all through your life. Yet honesty is the thing that makes us free. Once we have gotten all of the skeletons out of the closet and put them on the table where everyone can see them, no one can hurt us anymore. We have nothing to hide from anyone, and we can abandon the game of "Let's Pretend."

A great many of you may still be hiding. This is probably especially true with the boys who, at the senior high level, are usually convinced that they have a great deal more to lose if people find out what they are like. Men are supposed to be hard and tough; it is hard for a man to say, "I really need someone to appreciate me and care for me." Hopefully, however, you young men in the class have enough good experiences to make you say, "I wonder what it would be like if I would start telling people who I really am. Wouldn't it be better than pretending for the rest of my life?"

Probably very few of you have really learned to talk

and listen openly as yet, but this is not bad. Most people never learn this all of their lives. If the experiences that you have had here are going to have any meaning to you, it has to be just a beginning. It's very easy to slip back into the same habits of "Let's Pretend." Most of the people whom you associate with seldom really talk and listen.

One of the questions that is always asked at the end of a marriage program is: "What do you think of premarital sex? Is it as sinful as people say it is, if we really love each other?" I am always tempted to answer: "Yes, it is a terrible sin; you must behave." But this would not be honest. When I see the many reasons that young people have premarital sex, I wonder if, for most of them, it is any sin at all. Many young people know nothing about themselves or nothing about the person whom they are with. These people are driven by a curiosity that can be overwhelming. Some young people have been so deprived of love in their growing-up years that any decent treatment at all completely disarms them. Sin is something that you have to decide for yourselves; it is not something that any outsider can decide for you because he does not know you.

The sin that I am most concerned with in premarital sex is the sin that we commit against our marriage and our respect for each other. To me, premarital sex does not make very much sense. The way the span of life is increasing, those of you who are planning marriage are going to have to look at the same person across the breakfast table for forty or fifty years. I hope that you will love each other most of the time. Even if you do love each other, however, there will be times when you detest or even hate each other. This is human; and it is then that jealousy becomes a factor. The question occurs to you, "Does he (or she) really love me?"

I think that all of you already know how big a factor jealousy can be. How do you feel when the boy whom you really care about goes to the show with another girl? How do you feel when the girl whom you really like spends a lot of time talking to one of your best friends in the hall? I am sure that you all know enough about life and about yourselves to realize that when you live together for many years, you multiply these feelings of jealousy by a hundred or a thousand.

Premarital sex, to me, is senseless in another direction. It doesn't prove anything. The question is not whether it is right or wrong, but it is "Why?" Marriage is not a football game in which you study the plays and practice the moves.

My final and most important thought on premarital sex is difficult to express. Basically, I am trying to say that in marriage there is a feeling that "she is mine" and "I am hers." This feeling broadens and deepens as love grows. It is the meaning of "mine" that is so hard to explain. It always amuses me to hear some single person talk about the courage that it takes for married people to stay true to each other when there is so much temptation all around them. It is difficult to feel that we are "heroes" when there actually hasn't been any temptation for fifteen or twenty years. When love deepens and matures in marriage, there simply aren't any thoughts of sexual intercourse with another person. It is a mutually exclusive relationship. "I am hers, and she is mine." It does not make any sense at all for people who have lived this kind of love to upset it in any way. Yet, strangely enough, the love that a man feels for his wife helps him to respect, appreciate, and care about a lot of other women.

The question that all young people ask in their dating years is this: "If we cannot have sexual intercourse, how far should we go?" I can remember asking the same question myself as a young adult, and the whole idea of sex was so intriguing that I wanted to go as far as I could—and hopefully—maybe—someday someone would tell me that it was all right to go all the way. I wasn't very grown-up, and I wanted someone to make my decisions for me.

It is foolish to tell you how far you can go. Obviously you can go as far as you want to go. There is no way we can stop you. As young adults, the only real controls that you have are those that you build into yourselves. You have some choices to make between a few hours of fun—sexual experiences are always fun—and a lifetime of living together happily. It is your life; the choices are your own, as they are with every adult.

Yet, for those of you who are looking for direction, the question, "How far should we go?" is a serious one. For the immature person who thinks about boys or girls as those to be "conquered" or who is still engaging in the hurting kind of relations, it is no use talking about controls. Sex is not the problem. This person will want to reexamine himself and his feelings about men and women and why he behaves as he does.

For the rest of you, casual dating presents no problem. Limits are fairly easy to set. There is certainly some kissing and some necking (if you want). But I hope that even this will be honest. A kiss should always say, "I like you, and I appreciate your company." If it is an honest expression of liking and appreciation, there is nothing wrong and it is not phony.

For the serious couple who is "going steady" and is talking about marriage, we have an entirely different problem of limits. If you mean it, you had better be spending long hours together talking about everything that is important to the two of you. You had better want to be in each other's arms, and you had better spend some time in each other's arms. Your feelings are not wrong; they are good. But, how you handle these feelings will effect your entire life together.

Very soon your thoughts about yourselves, each other, and your marriage are going to bring you to the point where you have to decide whether you will have intercourse now or wait until you are married. Once you have made the decision, the limits become fairly clear-cut.

These limits are the sexual triggers. As we have mentioned in our chapter on "A Mature Sexuality," these include the tips of the breasts, French kissing, the vagina, and the clitoris of the woman; the thighs and penis of the man. Playing with these triggers is what you young people usually call "heavy petting." I think all of you are realistic enough to realize that when you play with a trigger, an explosion may occur.

It is possible, of course, for two young people to pet until one or both have reached a climax. Many young couples do. I cannot help feeling that this is "using" sex, and this practice brings no real fulfillment. It has two great dangers besides the frustration that it often brings. The first is that there is a complete breakdown in verbal communications. The second is that there is always the possibility that this relationship will not end as you intended it to end. It is very exciting, but often one or both parties feel drab, coarse, and used after it is over.

A certain amount of petting does occur, consciously or unconsciously, between any couple who is really in love. This is good and it is natural. Most of it is just a simple pressing of the bodies together to demonstrate love. The feelings that develop are difficult to handle, and this, too, is good. They can be handled through a solid, mature respect for each other and an honest relationship and dependency on God. The Man who built such wonderful feelings into sex and gave it such great rewards can certainly understand the feelings that He created.

Another question that we always get when we talk to high school students is this one: "How about those who already have? Does this mean that our chances for a successful marriage are ruined?" Of course not. Anyone who would say that seriously to you would be lying. I have suggested that premarital sexual intercourse does not make sense, and I truly believe that it does not. To me, it is a symbol of immaturity. Grown-up people ordinarily don't take those kind of risks with their future life.

But people do grow up, and many people who have had a great many premarital sexual experiences make excellent wives and husbands. But in each of these cases, the people involved have used these experiences to grow. Somewhere along the line, they have taken a hard look at themselves and asked themselves the honest question, "Why do I really behave as I do?"

Marriage will be a little harder for those who have already had sexual experiences. Jealousy will be a factor. But once the individual begins to understand himself, understanding his partner becomes easier, and the feelings of jealousy can be handled.

The question, "Is it really so wrong if we love each other?" is difficult to answer honestly. It is definitely just as wrong for people who have been married legally for years, to use sex as a weapon against each other. For people who say, "This is right because we love each other," I would wonder how mature their love really is. Is it real love or is it the feeling kind of love? If this is real love, and you really respect each other, then why is it impossible to wait to test this love in the real and permanent situation of marriage?

This brings us to some thoughts about the real meaning of adulthood. It does not mean that we act in an "adult fashion" all of the time. We are human beings and human beings do many foolish things. We get violently angry; we get drunk; we nag; we are sarcastic; and we hurt each other. We will be doing some of these things all through our lives.

Adulthood does mean that we accept responsibility for the things that we do. This whole question of accepting responsibility is something that you may want to think about again in closing. Perhaps some of you have blamed your parents because you find it difficult to communicate. Perhaps you are angry at your teachers because you have not received sex education, and you may have gotten into some trouble because of it. It is your life, and if these things have been wrong in your life, it will do little good to blame other people for them. You yourselves will have to correct them.

People go wrong; families go wrong; churches go wrong; governments go wrong; unions go wrong. They go wrong because the people who compose them gripe about the way they are run and refuse to accept any responsibility to change them. An outstanding example of this is the complete immaturity of the average Catholic layman who is constantly complaining about sisters, priests, and bishops; he does nothing to bring a more solid and useful Christianity into existence. Nothing is ever achieved that needs to be achieved unless we assume personal responsibility for achieving it.

Some people drop out of society. This is your choice. Many other people just exist. But all of the concepts that are worthwhile in life—democracy, freedom, Christianity, love—need change and require commitment and responsibility. Responsibility will help you look at yourself and like what you see.

DISCUSS

Classroom Discussion. I hope that your final discussion will be very personal. Both you, and the teacher who has gone through the program with you, should have developed a great deal of confidence and trust. If you have taken this program seriously, you are all very much aware of the tremendous personal growth that always takes place through open and honest communications. Most of you have learned to care deeply for other members of your class. Because the game of "Let's Pretend" is so deeply rooted in all of us, just about every member of the class is still going to have a great many "hangs-ups" that he is still hiding from. One of these people will be you. I think you would appreciate one of your friends telling you honestly about this hang-up that he sees in you, so that you can think about it and continue to grow as you leave this classroom. In turn, he will appreciate your telling him honestly exactly how you feel.

You may want to talk a little about your entire experience and what this is going to mean to you as you move out of the classroom and into ordinary life. The experience that you've come through with openness and honesty and the patterns that you have formed may not always make you more comfortable around other people. Many people resent openness because they don't know how to cope with it. Without even being aware that they are doing so, they may try to force you back into their little game of "Let's Pretend."

In preparing to meet this game, you might want to

analyze how important it has become to you to be able to live with yourself.

Discussion at Home. The program can help you to open communications in many areas. But it will not help you to continue and expand it. This you have to do yourself. Human beings are loaded with suspicions and fears, and it's very easy for all of us to slip back to the mind-reading, noncommunicating, hurt-feeling pattern. Because we are also afraid of ourselves, our first inclination in talking to people is to always present ourselves as a little better than we really are. We all have the very great tendency to avoid talking about things that may hurt.

I hope that your final discussion will be serious and quite realistic. When you face people as they are and learn to understand them, it becomes possible to love them.